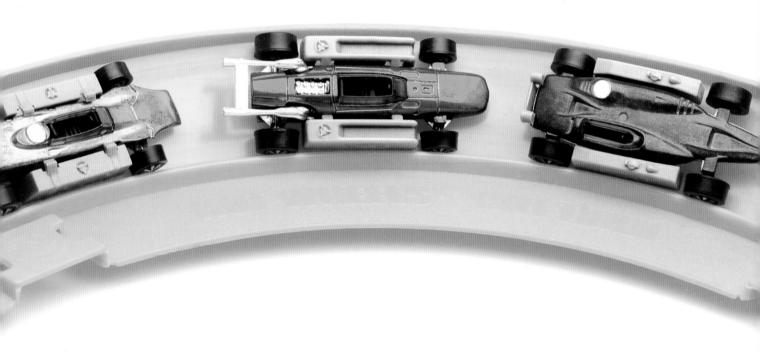

FROM 0 TO 50 AT 1:64 SCALE

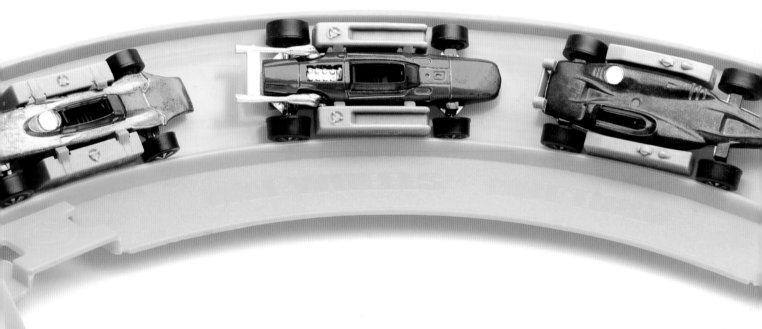

FROM 0 TO 50 AT 1:64 SCALE

Kris Palmer
Foreword by Larry Wood

motorbooks

Brimming with creative inspiration, how-to projects, and useful information to enrich your everyday life, Quarto Knows is a favorite destination for those pursuing their interests and passions. Visit our site and dig deeper with our books into your area of interest: Quarto Creates, Quarto Cooks, Quarto Homes, Quarto Lives, Quarto Drives, Quarto Explores, Quarto Gifts, or Quarto Kids.

First Published in 2018 by Motorbooks, an imprint of The Quarto Group.

401 Second Avenue North, Suite 310, Minneapolis, MN 55401 USA

T (612) 344-8100 **F** (612) 344-8691 **www.QuartoKnows.com**

Hot Wheels: From 0 to 50 at 1:64 Scale is produced by becker&mayer!, Bellevue, WA.

Motorbooks titles are also available at discount for retail, wholesale, promotional, and bulk purchase. For details, contact the Special Sales Manager by email at specialsales@quarto.com or by mail at The Quarto Group, Attn: Special Sales Manager, 401 Second Avenue North, Suite 310, Minneapolis, MN 55401 USA.

ISBN: 978-0-7603-6030-9

Author: Kris Palmer

Endsheet Art: Otto Kuhni

Editorial: Paul Ruditis and Delia Greve

Design: Scott Richardson

Photo Research: Farley Bookout and Daniel Perkins

Production: Tom Miller

225256

Printed in China

18 19 20 20 21 22   5 4 3 2 1

CONTENTS

50 YEARS OF HOT WHEELS

My dream job came through a party at the home of a friend, Howard Rees. We had worked together at Ford in Detroit before he came to Los Angeles. He invited me over when he learned that I had moved to L.A. too.

His kids were playing with little cars on orange track by the pool. I didn't have kids yet so I didn't recognize the toys, even though I'm a lifetime car nut. I asked Howard what they were. He said, "They're Hot Wheels. That's what I do." He added that he was leaving the position. I said, "Can you get me an interview?"

When I went in, human resources gave me an odd exam. They asked questions such as, "If you bent a piece of metal a particular way, what would it look like?" They were testing visualization, which was important for their designers. I must have done okay, because an executive then interviewed me.

He looked through my portfolio from Art Center and my work at Ford. Many of the designs were hand-built cars—hot rods and customs. That's what I loved. The executive liked them too. He called it the "California-custom" look. I didn't know it at the time, but he was the creator of Hot Wheels (and the "-el" in Mattel), Elliot Handler.

Elliot and his wife, Ruth, ran the company, but sometimes, for a change, she would check IDs at the building door. She was very protective of Mattel's toy ideas. Her rule was "no ID, no entry. Period." One day, she forgot her own ID and the guard wouldn't let her in. Rather than fire her, Ruth gave her a raise!

That family feel was cool. Everyone went by first names. We got together on weekends and went camping. If someone needed a hand, your Mattel friends were there. We worked hard and had fun too . . . pulling pranks. If you missed a day of work, you might find a mannequin on a toilet at your desk. One absentee returned to an office full of ladybugs. Another found a "Maintenance" sign attached to his door. His office was filled with mops and brooms.

And the work was rewarding. At an auto company, you might begin your career drawing door handles or badges. Mattel wanted the whole car. Tri-Baby was my first design, incorporating a jet turbine—an idea I got from doing some work with Pratt & Whitney. Another of my favorites is Purple Passion. Its styling is similar to a '49 Mercury, one of the cars frequently featured in hot rod magazines when I was kid. Purple Passion's success proved that collectors were interested in Hot Wheels. The enclosed rear wheels scraped the track-side, so it wasn't the fastest model—but fans liked the look and it became very popular.

When I started, Mattel's six-story building in Hawthorne was 90 percent Barbie. But work by designers like Harry Bentley Bradley, Ira Gilford, Howard Rees, and my work—which I did for 40 years—pushed Hot Wheels to the top of the die-cast car world, and that continues to build with terrific new designers.

Never in my wildest dreams, 49 years ago, would I have thought that the little cars I was drawing would have lasted and been so successful. Thanks to everyone who made them such an iconic piece of Americana!

Larry R. Wood.

Opposite: *Larry Wood hard at work sketching a new Hot Wheels design, 1969.*

Chapter 1

RISING TO THE CHALLENGE

Hot Wheels is the number–one selling toy in the world—not just the best-selling toy car. Achieving that number-one status was built on creativity and determination. The visionary behind the toy was a man who did not back down from a challenge. Elliot Handler was the son of a painter, who grew up in a working-class neighborhood of Denver, Colorado.

When Handler had the idea for a better toy car, the market for die-cast vehicles was neither underdeveloped nor considered vulnerable. Rather, by the mid-1960s, play cars were a solid presence in stores and being produced by manufacturers of international renown. The Mattel Company, founded in 1945, had seen great success with Barbie dolls, but the plan to create a car with superior styling and speed was vague. In-house departments had varying degrees of optimism and enthusiasm for the project. Even Ruth Handler, the company's second-in-command, had reservations.

Yet Elliot Handler was unwavering. He had faith in his designers, his company, and its methods. He knew they would overcome any obstacle or disadvantage.

The Mattel team came through, big. The cars, tracks, and play sets that emerged from Mattel's battle against the odds are now sold worldwide. From sixteen original models, the list has grown to thousands with billions of fans around the world.

The race- and stunt- and trick-filled world has been refined and expanded upon by thousands of employees. The line now includes vehicles of all types, custom rides, and fantasy speedsters—from showrooms and racetracks to movies, cartoons, and comic books. The lines feature cars smaller than a book of matches, as well as life-size working vehicles and many scales in-between.

Nearly everyone has heard of Hot Wheels, and a vast number grew up racing and loving them. But that success did not come easy. Nor is designing, making, shipping, and selling the toys around the world a simple job. Toys are a competitive market with new technologies emerging annually. Staying relevant and exciting while maintaining high quality year after year is a ceaseless and stimulating challenge—a challenge the Mattel team has conquered time and again.

Opposite: Self-powered Sizzlers offered a break from gravity—and also a "speed brake" accessory, used to slow the cars just enough to keep them on the track. (Early advertising photo used by Mattel, 1970.)

SEARCH FOR THE
MISSING MOJO

Opportunity wasn't knocking. How could it be? According to Mattel's marketing department, the opportunity wasn't there—not locally, not in California, not in the United States, nor anywhere in the world. In the 1960s, there was no opportunity in toy cars. It was a glutted market.

That opinion was wrong, but Elliot Handler couldn't know that at the time. He was the "-el" in Mattel and the president of the operation. He listened to his experts' analysis, and he told them they were going forward anyway.

In his soul, Elliot was an artist. His sense for what customers would find appealing was broader than data—also more ambiguous. He trusted his instincts, which were pulling his mind to this concept. His instincts had led him to Ruth and the formation of the company they ran together. With her at his side, they would make his idea work.

If there was no opportunity in toy cars as currently conceived, Mattel would offer something different. They would ignite a demand no other manufacturer had foreseen. That's what Mattel did best.

Cause for hope did exist. Toys that engaged children's minds and connected them to the world could endure for millennia. Consider the humble ball. It probably evolved from stones thrown at rivals or prey, where contact was key—miss, and your quarry either ran or introduced you to some teeth and claws or another rock. To improve their aim, our ancestors practiced throwing and discovered it was fun. People eventually broadened the play with bats, racquets, sticks, and slings.

Other immortal toys likewise possessed some enduring relevance to nature's workings. Tops reduced physics to cribside form, standing while they spun, toppling when they slowed. Surely some of history's

Left: Jack Ryan observes a test launch of Mattel's Super-Thrust H_2O Two-Stage Missile Set, circa 1958. **Right:** Toy guns were big business in the late 1950s, including Mattel's highly realistic, Western-style, Fanner cap guns, with firing toy bullets, shown here with Jack Ryan.

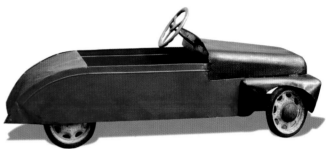

inventors were inspired by the rotational forces involved. Kites rode the wind, a force that could push sails and turn windmills, while dolls reduced large and potentially intimidating humans to a quiet, approachable form.

Ruth's tour de force had hit that evolutionary sweet spot, taking an existing toy in a new direction. A doll styled like a young woman, rather than a little child, with a wardrobe all her own was a distinction that made Barbie a household name.

Miniature vehicles were likewise a proven concept. By the early 1960s, play cars were as ubiquitous in toy stores as balls, kites, tops, and dolls. Yet shrinking an object to handheld size is not the same as creating an exciting toy. Though these automotive reproductions looked like their full-size counterparts, there was room for something more. Elliot knew it in his gut, and he was determined to find the key to make Mattel's little car a sensation.

Left: The Barbie doll, like this brunette "No. 1 Barbie" from 1959, was shaped like a young woman rather than a baby. **Right:** The toy market before Hot Wheels included overly simplistic or very realistic-looking cars that could not move on their own, such as these two vintage toy cars. **Next page:** A group of children gaze at toys on sale in a London department store, circa 1930.

RUTH AND ELLIOT

What Ruth Mosko wanted, she usually got—mostly from hard work and her indomitable spirit. With Elliot, then known as "Izzy," the universe was more generous. She first saw him on a Denver sidewalk from the seat of her new '32 Ford. His mane of dark, curly locks captured her attention on sight.

Later, when she went to a charity dance, he was there. He looked at her like she was the one he had come to meet. Dances were a nickel apiece, and Elliot borrowed from friends to monopolize Ruth all night.

They were opposites in the perfect complementary way. She was a businesswoman in search of worthy commodities, and he was an artist, looking to produce innovative works for a broad audience. Handler's creativity, which encompassed an uncanny vision for what the public might favor, was ideally paired to Mosko's relentless drive to find investors, facilities, machines—any resource the couple needed to wedge their way into the marketplace.

Ruth was the youngest of ten children and the only one not raised by her biological parents. She had been cared for by her

Top: Ruth and Elliot Handler, founders of Mattel, circa 1960. **Bottom:** Early products from Elliot Handler Plastics included items such as this lucite bunny lamp.

DESTINED TO THRIVE

eldest sister, Sarah, from the time their mother entered the hospital for surgery when Ruth was six months old. Their mother came home and recovered, but Ruth remained with her sister.

Sarah had a strong business sense and a responsible husband in Louis Greenwald. They worked hard, saved money, and brought up Ruth with amenities that her siblings didn't have—like the Ford coupe from which she spied Elliot.

Elliot had no such security. He was a painter's son from a poorer section of Denver who often wore the same torn white T-shirt when he went to meet Ruth. Sarah disapproved, but not because of Elliot's character. She feared for Ruth's financial future dating an aspiring artist.

But Ruth did not need a provider. She needed Elliot. And he needed her. They married in Denver on June 26, 1938, and moved to Los Angeles. En route, she asked him to use his middle name, Elliot (rather than Izzy, short for Isadore), for their future life. He agreed, following his simple principle: "As long as she's happy, I'm happy."

Top: The original Mattel Creations building, established in 1945. **Bottom:** Ruth and Elliot Handler, 1937.

While Ruth worked as a stenographer at Paramount Studios, Elliot took classes at the Art Center College of Design. A teacher had the class working with a durable, clear plastic, made by DuPont as Lucite, and Rohm and Haas as Plexiglas. Most of it went to the aviation industry for windscreens and turrets. Elliot's instructor wanted students to try it for commercial products.

Elliot walked around the couple's apartment, surveying for items he could fabricate in the new plastic. He sketched out lamps and ashtrays and showed them to Ruth. She said if he could make the items, she would sell them.

They bought equipment from Sears and set up shop in the garage they shared with another tenant at their apartment complex. When the other resident complained about the dust, they found their own tiny shop. Elliot asked Harold "Matt" Matson, a friend he met while working for a lighting company, to make them a new oven to shape plastics. The Handlers borrowed from friends and family and employed their small savings to stay afloat.

When Elliot had produced an assortment of cigarette boxes, hand mirrors, bookends, and other small pieces, Ruth loaded them into a case and took them to work. On her lunch break, she drove to Zacho's, a gift shop on Wilshire Boulevard, where she asked to see the owner. Mr. Zacho was impressed, but he wanted to check out their shop before ordering.

Zacho arrived that Saturday at Elliot Handler Plastics, a tiny converted storefront laundry. After a brief look around, he placed an order that Elliot wrote out on a torn piece of packing paper. The $500 order was worth five years of shop rent!

Above: Elliot's costume-jewelry creations caught the eye of investor Zachary Zemby. Elzac, the company combining their names, employed large-scale production with some three hundred employees. Here, workers are shown painting figurines.

Their sale was proof of concept: Ruth could entice retailers with her business acumen; Elliot could craft goods that shoppers wanted to own. They reinvested their earnings and pushed ahead.

An entrepreneur named Zachary Zemby had seen Elliot's work and was impressed. He offered to form a partnership, provide the funds, and write ad copy. The resulting company, Elzac, combined their names and resources. He also employed Matt Matson.

Elzac introduced the Handlers to a large-scale operation as well as the friction that sharing decisions with others can create. By 1944, Elzac had some three hundred employees, $2 million in annual sales, and a disgruntled lead designer, Elliot.

Matson was unhappy too. He left Elzac, and approached Elliot, asking for permission to produce

and sell some of his designs. Ruth offered to look for buyers and secured a sizeable initial order from a store called Austin Photography Studios.

Soon Elliot was also ready to leave Elzac. In October 1944, the Handlers met at Matt Matson's house and formed a new company, combining the latter's nickname and the first two letters of Elliot to form *Mattel*.

Matson later sold out to Sarah and Louis Greenwald, and the company shifted its emphasis to toys, including music boxes, dolls, instruments, play guns, and eventually cars. But the Mattel name—and Ruth and Elliot's consuming passion for success—remained. Over the next two decades, the couple who had met through a sidewalk glance and a nickel dance would build Mattel into the largest toy company in the world.

Above: Elzac creations utilized a variety of materials, such as plastic and wood as seen in the creation of this bull pin. **Next pages:** These toy displays of the 1950s and 1960s show how Mattel toys broke the mold. Prior to Mattel, toy vehicles were bigger and less detailed, while dolls featured the proportions of a young child.

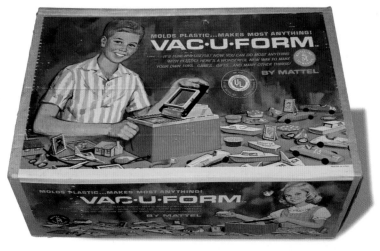

Dear Mom: If he wears out a pair of perfectly good shoes in two months, and his jeans go through at the knees in no time, and he leaves you limp by 7 p.m.....ask Dad to get him something he can't wear out: a bike by <u>Mattel</u>!

Dear Dad: Mattel's new V-RROOM!® BRONCO 20″ bicycle is the toughest bike under the son—with heavy-duty shock absorbers, a front pivot, to take the bounce out of bumps, a double frame of rugged chrome steel, a Bendix coaster brake, and reinforced wheels with extra spokes. Oh yes: plus Mattel's optional V-RROOM! sound unit with the roar that makes like a motorcycle! And it's rough-'n-tough enough for *you* to ride!

Mattel took an open-minded, far-reaching approach to its market. Designers were encouraged to let their imaginations go wherever inspiration took them. These offerings from the 1960s show that range. Barbie accessories proved wildly successful. The mid-1960s Linoprinter, Vac-u-form, Fright Factory, Creepy Crawlers, and Fun Flowers kits encouraged kids to create, as Mattel did. The V-RROOM Bronco bicycle offered motorcycle styling with engine noise. The Ken doll arrived in 1961, while Skipper was introduced in 1964 as Barbie's younger sister. See 'n' Say spoke to children, literally.

SOME ROCKET SCIENCE REQUIRED

Elliot was at odds with his marketing people. They had investigated the toy car market and were not encouraged. Stores were already filled with miniatures by Matchbox, Husky, Budgie, Dinky, and others. Matchbox had entered the $\frac{1}{64}$-scale market a decade earlier in 1953. To marketing, Mattel had missed its chance by nearly a generation.

Beyond shelf space and freshness, there was also the big numbers hurdle. By the mid-'60s, established toy manufacturers were turning out tens of millions of cars per year, upon which toy retailers expended a hefty portion of their product budget. With that level of influence by existing players, Mattel's skeptics wondered how a late entrant would get a meaningful market share.

Elliot had a different perspective. The products he and Ruth had sold through their original company, Elliot Handler Plastics, were also common items. Everyone had lamps and ashtrays and candleholders and picture frames. Those goods didn't respond to some vacuum in the marketplace. Rather, they lured buyers away from existing products. Had he and Ruth failed with that approach, there would be no Mattel.

By this period, Mattel was a dominant player in the world toy market. And one of its greatest hits had been a type of toy that had been around not just for a generation, but for millennia: the Barbie doll developed by Ruth and named after their first child, Barbara.

By any measure, the Handlers were an especially driven, hardworking pair—the children of immigrants, impassioned to achieve better lives for themselves and their colleagues. They were quick learners and risk-takers, willing to gamble big on ideas they felt had high play value. Mattel reflected their personal drive.

They recruited the brightest, most creative, most highly motivated people they could find and encouraged an intimate, collaborative atmosphere. Mattel used first names at all levels. Its workforce was also highly diverse. The Los Angeles Conference on Community Relations had compared a visit to the factory in the 1950s to a tour of the United Nations. There were more women than men on the production line, of all colors, backgrounds, and religions. Management hired elderly applicants too, and those with disabilities.

Above: This 1967 concept sketch of a Mustang designed by Harry Bradley shows off the look Mattel settled upon for its new toy—a real-car feel with touches like hood scoops, mag wheels, wide tires that were larger in the rear, and side pipes.

Elliot was confident that this bright, broad-minded company could make a toy car to beat the market. Mattel's offering would not simply sit alongside the millions of toy cars already in stores but displace them. Part of his drive was personal. He and Ruth had devoted their lives to the toy business, and their grandson's favorite plaything was a little car not made by Mattel.

To accelerate development, Elliot would unleash several creative minds on a problem simultaneously. They were encouraged to take their own approach, seeking fresh insights—yet also to share any breakthroughs with other groups working on a project. In this way, Mattel condensed the refinement process and brought better toys to market faster than its competitors.

Within their talent pool was Jack Ryan, a Yale-trained engineer who had worked at the defense contractor Raytheon Company designing missile systems. Ruth and Elliot made him head of Mattel's preliminary design department, accepting his demand that he receive royalties for products he designed. He would go on to hold more than a thousand patents and play an important role in many of Mattel's successes.

The Handlers also put Jack Barcus of Mattel's research and development department on the project. Like Ryan, Barcus added sharp minds from his group to brainstorm a revolutionary toy car.

Fred Adickes from industrial design was in on the game too. He had come from Chrysler and was well-versed in full-size cars. Mattel sent him back to Detroit to recruit additional capable car folks.

Adickes interviewed Harry Bentley Bradley, who had been designing cars for General Motors for two years after obtaining a Stanford master's degree in engineering. Bradley didn't know much about Mattel, but he was interested in California. If the toy company job fell flat, he hoped to land something at one of the Japanese car companies setting up U.S. headquarters on the West Coast. He viewed Japan's cars as efficient and well-made yet lacking in style.

Apparently, Mattel had been vague about what, exactly, Bradley would be doing there. This could have been due to Mattel's secrecy about new products. Not until Bradley arrived for work in Los Angeles in October 1966 did he learn what his new employer wanted him to design. He was surprised. If the connection between full-size and handheld automobiles was obvious to Elliot and Adickes, it wasn't plain to Bradley. He wasn't sure what would make a toy car appealing to the masses.

Right: The big influences the small in production and design. Automation, experimental styling, and computer processing evolved for major car companies' production as well as for Hot Wheels' and Mattel's plants.

Adickes and Bradley started by studying what was already on the market, because Elliot wanted to raise the bar above the competition. They secured examples of every play car they could find at toy stores and dime stores around L.A. The total was a couple hundred, which Adickes and a marketing planner, Len Mayem, wired to rolling display boards so Bradley and the other designers could maneuver them about and study their design. A few things stood out as improvable: some of the castings were primitive; paint schemes were drab and uninspired; and the level of detail varied from impressionistic to recognizably accurate.

While designers worked on the new toy's looks, Ryan, Barcus, and their selected employees tinkered with engineering concepts in search of something fresh. Mattel's assignment with both elements was to have a spectacular product to debut at Toy Fair, in New York City. The small toys they came up with were brightly colored and "jacked up," with wide tires and mag wheels. Some resembled actual production cars, while others were wild and distinct. They all rolled well. Quite well.

Marketers thought the company might secure orders for five million cars the first year, a 10 percent share of the market. Elliot believed they could do better.

Left: Elliot and Ruth enjoy the fruits of their labors, playing with Sizzlers, introduced in 1970. **Top right:** Corgi Toys' vehicles were the popular toy cars of the early 1960s, but they were not speedy. **Bottom right:** Prior to Hot Wheels, wheeled toys rolled for convenience, not for excitement.

TOY FAIR OR BUST

Mattel was a manufacturer, not a retailer. Thus, its initial market was not parents or kids browsing department-store aisles but the corporate buyers who determined what toys would stock those aisles. A large order from Kmart, JC Penney, or Sears, Roebuck & Company could make a toy a household name. A tepid response could kill the product.

Toy manufacturers had been toting their wares to New York City since at least 1894. In that year, Madison Square Garden hosted The Great Toy Exhibition, which promoters referred to as a toy fair. It was designed to emulate the streets of Nuremberg, the German city famous for its toys. More than a hundred shops featured creations from around the world, accented with music and shows that inspired journalists to call the event a "fairyland for children."

In 1903 a similarly intensive promotion also took the name Toy Fair; however, this incarnation, which continues to this day, was limited to those in the toy industry. It was the premier toy-debut event, and the one Elliot and his innovators meant to wow.

The Toy Fair of March 1968 would include fifteen thousand buyers ready to make purchases for the year ahead. Mattel hedged its bets by inviting Ken Sanger, from Kmart, out to L.A. for a sneak preview of its new little cars. Bernie Loomis, VP of sales, had a special room set up with two strips of track, raised on one end, running down the floor. He had a whole presentation prepared for Sanger, but when the guest of honor arrived, Loomis let the product speak for itself. He held up a Matchbox car, which Sanger had said was important to his employer.

Loomis released it on the track and it rambled down a bit and fell off. Then he held up a Hot Wheels prototype, with its bright paint, high level of detail, and customized touches. He said it was "something new."

Loomis released Mattel's car, and they watched as it shot down the track, off the end, and across the floor. All eyes then snapped to Sanger. Toy Fair was just ahead, and his impression was a reliable indicator of whether they had any hope of meeting marketing's projection for first-year sales. Sanger expressed regret at the order he had in mind. "Keep it short," he said, "at fifty million."

Fifty million! A single buyer wanted *ten* times marketing's prediction, an amount equal to the total existing market for toy cars.

Elliot had his verdict: "Hot Wheels" were just that.

Above: Ruth and Elliot show off Hot Wheels at the Paris toy show in 1970. Hot Wheels, with their tailor-made racetracks, were a hot commodity.

COIN OPERATED BATTERY CAB

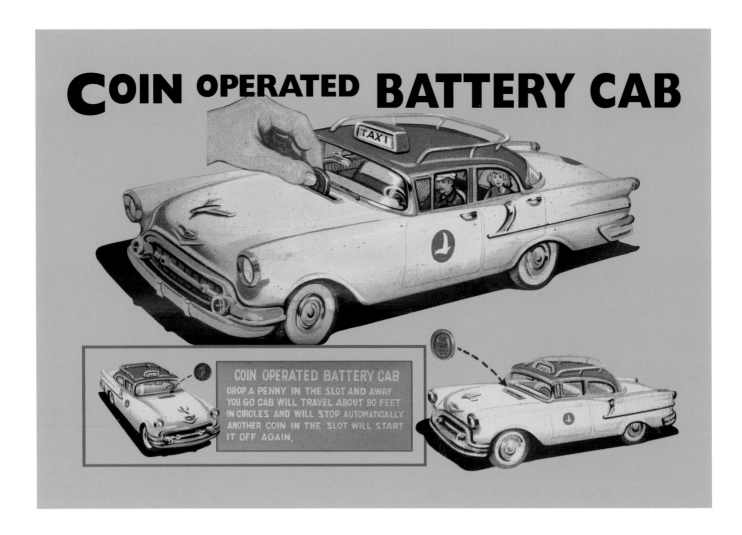

COIN OPERATED BATTERY CAB
DROP A PENNY IN THE SLOT AND AWAY
YOU GO CAB WILL TRAVEL ABOUT 90 FEET
IN CIRCLES AND WILL STOP AUTOMATICALLY
ANOTHER COIN IN THE SLOT WILL START
IT OFF AGAIN.

To attack its new project, Mattel recruited designers from Detroit. It was obvious to the toymaker that the epicenter of the U.S. automotive industry was the right place to find the necessary talent. To the designers planning out human conveyances, however, the connection was hazy at best. What was a staple of their adult existence in a vast nation, was like a child's toy in name only. Era toys, such as these on the left, lacked the styles and presence of the full-size vehicles seen in these automobile ads from the 1950s and 1960s. Mattel's goal was to change that.

'54 Plymouth

On this page you see the beauty of it.
On the next page you see some of the other 5t it.

Starfire ...AN OLDSMOBILE ORIGINAL

There's **SOMETHING EXTRA** about owning an OLDS!

From Ford USA: the elegant new Galaxie for 1962

The trend-making Galaxie is the world's easiest-to-own luxury car, and every Galaxie includes in its low Ford price advanced-design body features other cars will not have until tomorrow, for this is the fine car that's beautifully built to be more service-free.

There's "SOMETHING EXTRA" about owning an OLDS!

NEW FOR '62 . . . F-85 Cutlass Convertible featuring foam-padded bucket seats, de luxe steering wheel, padded instrument panel, power top—plus ultra high-compression Cutlass 185-h.p. aluminum V-8 engine. Also shown: F-85 Cutlass Coupe.

Announcing for '62!

OLDSMOBILE'S
Fun-to-drive F-85 →
featuring a new Cutlass Convertible!

In a class by itself... in the low-price field!

For '62 ... every F-85 has that "something extra" you expect in an Oldsmobile! Call it fun ... adventure ... excitement! Notice it in the fine styling and craftsmanship that put this Olds in a class by itself ... in the low-price field! Experience it in the exciting performance from zippy aluminum V-8 engines—with up to 185 high-compression horsepower ... and in the smooth new "feel" of 4-S HYDRA-MATIC*, the

performance transmission! You'll also enjoy easy handling and parking ... new rear-seat roominess in sedan models ... reassuring Oldsmobile roadability ... steady, softer-than-ever ride. Choose from a full line of F-85 models—sedans, coupes, wagons and sparkling convertibles! There's a fun-loving F-85 sized right ... powered right ... priced right for you!

OLDSMOBILE DIVISION • GENERAL MOTORS CORPORATION *Optional extra cost.

TOY-SIZED CAR

By the early 1960s, Mattel was selling millions of playthings to children around the world. Gross annual sales were climbing toward $100 million. Elliot Handler was the president of the company, and he wanted to make a toy car. It seemed simple enough, but the challenge came in answering the equally basic question: What is a "toy car"?

Everyone knew what cars were, but cars were not toys. They were large machines used to transport people and objects. You needed money to buy one, a license to drive it, fuel to operate it, maintenance to keep it running, and ample space to operate and store it. These realities were not fun, and they were not play.

Sure, cars are fun to drive—to climb into and rocket across the landscape. But the technology to reduce an actual automobile to miniature size, with functioning drivetrain, brakes, and fuel and electrical systems did not exist, at least not with a budget smaller than the Apollo program's. And even if Mattel's geniuses accomplished the feat, the smallest child could not sit in a thimble-size passenger compartment to make it go like a real car.

As former GM designer Harry Bradley learned, an automobile for the adult world was at best only hazy inspiration for a plaything that would interest kids. Yet opportunity waited quietly within the differences. While toy cars could not mimic the genuine article's qualities, a tiny object *could* do things that aren't possible with a full-size vehicle.

To start, what child's toy has not been dropped during play? A tiny car fumbled from a child's height is like a full-size version driving off a building. Gravity may punish one of them with a scratch. The other it will damage beyond repair, if not beyond recognition.

Above: This full-size Austin Westminster A105 next to its smaller toy counterpart made by Dinky Toys makes clear the lack of detail carried through to other toy cars.

In, up and out of thrilling 360° loop

OR CAR-SHAPED TOY?

How about a jump, like in movies and shows? Watch *Bullitt* or *Dukes of Hazzard* in slow motion and you will glimpse how a ton-and-a-half of steel fares when it slams into the ground after a brief flight. Suspensions bottom out, frames bend, and fenders buckle. Production reportedly consumed more than a hundred Chargers to capture Bo and Luke Duke leaping bridges and barns to escape Boss Hogg and his cronies.

Nature's forces pose a feeble threat at handheld scale and are easily overcome. In a kid's hand, cars can defy gravity, driving up walls or along the undersides of tables—feats that would take huge machines or special effects artists to match with a real automobile.

Other distinctions also play to a child's and parent's advantage. Real cars require maintenance over time, even those that aren't driven. Playing with several cars from a full-size collection can take hours, depending on when they were last run. Tires deflate, batteries die, fluids leak, gas turns gummy, and pests take up residence. These are never toy car problems.

By the 1960s, there were hundreds of models and millions of examples of tiny cars on the market. Some of them looked remarkably like their full-size counterparts. That fact alone did nothing to stop Mattel from crashing the party with a hot rod–shaped wrecking ball.

Kids wanted play value more than authenticity. Even if a vehicle's appearance affected children's initial interest, it was the toy's ability to zoom and jump and sail and crash, again and again, in ways no adult car could withstand, that set Mattel's little die-cast apart from—and a long way ahead of—the rest.

Above: Images from a 1968 advertisement for the Stunt Action set showcased Hot Wheels gravity-defying abilities.

Chapter 2

SPEED BY DESIGN

To confront an established market like die-cast cars, Mattel needed something its competitors weren't offering. It had to be a fresh trait—something outstanding. Up until Ken Sanger placed his order for Kmart, Elliot and his team weren't positive they had it right. Yet from the beginning, Mattel's designers knew more than they realized. Beyond their walls, out in the world, there was a revered quality ready to lend a hand, a quality that made names famous across sports and across species—names like Chuck Yeager, Jim Thorpe, Jesse Owens, Wilma Rudolph, greyhound, and cheetah.

The main ingredient was speed. It was cool to be fast. It was cooler to *look* fast.

When Mattel decided to enter the toy car market, the established players didn't care about speed. A few small cars by Matchbox, Budgie, or Husky drew inspiration from racing. And those "race cars" didn't roll any faster than the milk trucks and farm tractors on adjacent shelves. The hot-rod and speed culture flourishing outside toy stores' display windows had not yet been invited inside.

Opposite: Playing with cars in the driveway was a vibe Mattel could tap into. These California young men removed parts that hindered speed and improved those that helped it. **Right:** Drag racing was a wild, loud, collaborative, competitive scene, attractive to youth—characteristics that Hot Wheels aimed to capture.

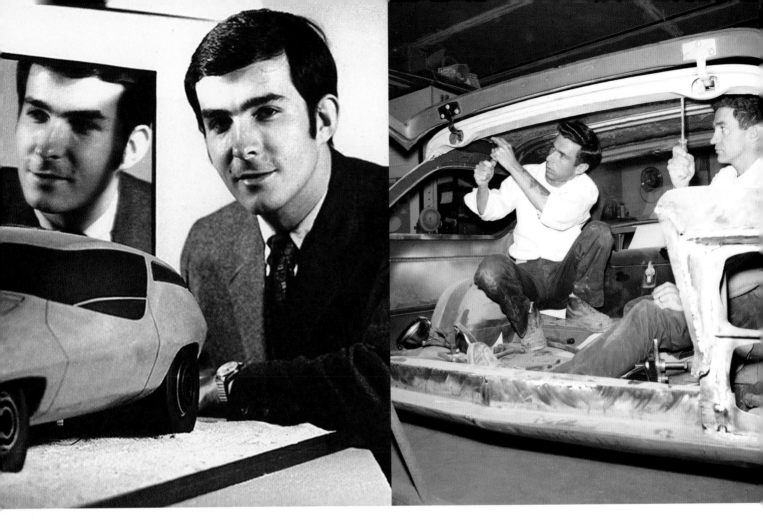

Clues to solve the speed mystery were present at Mattel—right by the door, in fact. Harry Bradley walked with crutches, so the company had given him a prime parking space when he arrived. He drove a bright yellow 1964 Chevy El Camino modified by Alexander Brothers Custom Shop in Detroit. It had five-spoke mag wheels, redline tires, mock velocity stacks bursting from the hood, and a raked, free-rolling stance from its raised back end. Bradley's ride looked fast, yet Mattel did not internalize it . . . not right away.

Another asset awaiting discovery had a less obvious connection to speed, except maybe to an engineer. It was a spool of mandolin wire, ordered from New Jersey for an earlier project Mattel had tried to develop—a play guitar that did not go out of tune. The wire was too expensive for the company to hit its price point for the instrument, so the project was abandoned and the pricey spool went on a shelf.

A mandolin string has little in common with a car axle, unless you're thinking in miniature scale—say, around 1/64. In that event, a consistent, high-quality, thin wire might get your wheels turning, both figuratively and literally.

The competition's ground game was primitive, with bulky steel rods used as axles in most toy cars. The metal pins were placed through a hole in a simple plastic-disk wheel and were flattened on the ends to hold it in place. This coarse construction permitted rolling that was like a shopping cart at best.

Elliot and Ruth demanded high quality and consistency in their products, for which the foundation was set in preliminary design. When Jack Ryan's team scrutinized the competition, its mediocre motion cried out. Wheels' enduring purpose was to reduce the work required to move an object. Well-designed rollers spun freely—the more freely, the better to do their job. The plodding disks on existing toy cars left much room for improvement.

Top left: Designer Harry Bentley Bradley knew cars, not toys. Elliot saw no problems there. **Top right:** The Alexander brothers, at their custom shop in Detroit, work to build Bradley's 1964 El Camino.

Fellow engineer Jack Malek proposed that the fine mandolin wire from the guitar project could provide a smaller rolling surface and reduce friction against the wheel. Inserting a bearing would make it spin faster still. Although the scale was too small for ball bearings, a low-friction bushing would speed things up. The obvious material here was plastic, an industry Mattel watched closely as a toymaker. Another engineer, Howard Newman, identified Delrin, a DuPont product, as an excellent low-friction material to turn against the axle.

For a final tweak, design reshaped the wheels, giving them a subtle taper from the inside to the outside and adding a thin ridge to the inner edge. This trick shrank the rolling gear's contact patch with the ground to a mere speck—the minute portion of the inner ridge that touched the track. The adjustment reduced rolling resistance without spoiling the wide-tire look.

With its subtly pared, bearing-loaded wheels turning on two mandolin-wire axles, engineering's prototypes hauled asphalt. The axle design also had flex, like a real suspension, so that the cars sprung up if pushed downward and the front or rear bounced if lifted and dropped. The demo toys felt taut, lively, and packed with play value.

To this undercarriage built for speed, Mattel would add a variety of body styles penned by Bradley and colleagues, inspired by the bright colors and go-fast aura of his customized El Camino.

Top right: Success builds on itself. Uke-a-Doodle, a playable ukulele with an internal music box, was Mattel's first hit. **Bottom:** Mattel's breakaway car's performance came from its unique wheels, set upon fine axles, with low-friction bearings, rolling on a thin lip at the wheels' inner edges.

'32 Ford roadtest 4 vs. V8!!

ROD & Custom

JULY 1968 50¢ UK 4/3 Sweden KR 3.95 (ink)

DESIGN ENGINEER'S

'29 PHAETON

HOT ROD MATH
by Jim McFarland

LOW COST VW CAM INSTALLATION

from JUNK to RESTORED to STREET ROD

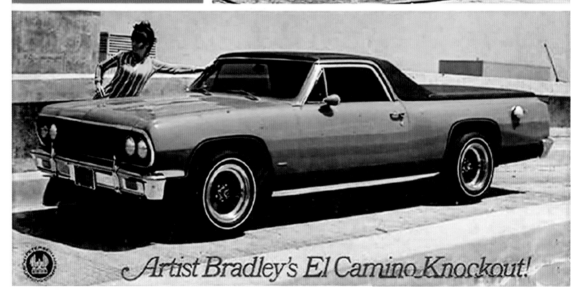

Artist Bradley's El Camino Knockout!

Sometimes a great idea is not hidden in abstraction, waiting for a genius to extract it. It's sitting in plain sight. Bradley's Deora and custom El Camino had wowed crowds on car-show floors and magazine covers. Mattel captured that styling with a high level of detail and certain modifications—like removing the shut lines from the El Camino's doors and rounding the wheel arches to allow suspension movement without interference—seen in the 4x scale prototype (bottom left) and the $\frac{1}{64}$-scale versions (top and middle left). Custom cars would be a staple of the Hot Wheels line.

REALITY RODDED, ORIGINALS UNBOUND

The first batch of Hot Wheels released in 1968 combined designs evoking production models from Detroit, a Ford race car, a typical hot rod, and more original conceptions derived from custom builders and the designers' diverse inspirations. This debut generation is known as the "Sweet Sixteen": Custom Mustang, Custom Cougar, Custom Corvette, Custom Fleetside, Custom Camaro, Custom Barracuda, Custom T-Bird, Custom Firebird, Custom Volkswagen, and Custom Eldorado, plus Python (née Cheetah), Beatnik Bandit, Hot Heap, Ford J-Car, Silhouette, and Deora.

They boast fast-rolling wheels and thin-wire axles for actual speed, plus a "jacked-up" back end, due to bigger rear wheels, to enhance the performance-car look. Cheetah, Silhouette, Beatnik Bandit, and Hot Heap have exposed chromed engines, as does the Custom Volkswagen (Beetle), uncharacteristically placed up front. Most of the production-based vehicles feature custom exhaust pipes exiting behind the front wheels. Every version was available in bright, Spectraflame paint, which was applied over die-cast bodies without primer to allow the underlying zinc-plated metal to shine through.

Custom Fleetside was inspired by Bradley's custom El Camino. He had owned it since his days at General Motors and parked it daily outside Mattel's design studios while Bradley and other designers sought inspiration. Early sketches from the toy car team had not been hitting the right vibe for Elliot. Finally, grasping for a reference, Elliot told Bradley to draw something like that thing he parked out front. Fittingly, the Alexander brothers knew that vehicle as Blind Faith.

With that focal point established, the creative floodgates opened. The Hot Wheels Custom Fleetside was a straightforward application of Elliot's advice, taking Bradley's car and replicating it at a smaller scale. Bradley also penned customized miniatures based on Barracuda, Corvette, Camaro, Firebird, Eldorado, Cougar, Mustang, T-Bird, and American Motors' AMX—although Mattel did not include the AMX among its Sweet Sixteen.

Bradley sketched the Silhouette and Hot Heap based on real cars by Bill Cushenberry and Don Tognotti, respectively, and the Beatnik Bandit after the full-size custom from Ed Roth. The J-Car he modeled on Ford's racing GT40 Mark IV. The front-engined Beetle was a design Bradley created with Ira Gilford, who would go on to pen several other iconic early Hot Wheels. Deora emulated a Dodge full-size show truck designed by Bradley and built, like Blind Faith, by Alexander Brothers Custom Shop in Detroit.

Today, the Python is as interesting to collectors for its design as it is for its name. Dean Jeffries is credited with the Hot Wheels version. Like the Silhouette, it was based on a Cushenberry full-size car. Mattel originally called its miniature Cheetah but changed the name because a GM executive used that moniker for his Corvette race car. The very few early Hot Wheels labeled Cheetah, rather than Python, are now prized collectibles.

Several origin stories have carried down the decades describing how this fast, funky fleet came to be called Hot Wheels. One version is that Elliot saw Bradley's El Camino in the parking lot and called it a set of "hot wheels." Another credits the term to Elliot's exclamation when Jack Ryan sped a demo car across Elliot's desk. A third take is that Alexandra Laird, Mattel's "namesmith," wrote out a number of proposed titles for the little cars, one of which was "Big Wheels." Elliot generally liked that one but wanted a word other than "big." He and Laird ran through variations together and agreed that "Hot Wheels" sounded best.

Which use was the first is hard to prove a half century later. Elliot could have said "hot wheels" in any of these settings or all of them, with Bradley, Ryan, and Laird each reasonably believing that it was the original coining.

Above: Designer Harry Bradley's drawing of a 1967 Thunderbird. After much trial and error, the design team settled on the essential Hot Wheels look, to which any style of car could be adapted to fit in the line.

FORD "J" CAR / COMPETITION CAR   ©MATTEL INC.   H. BRADLEY   7-8-6

Above: Harry Bradley's drawing of a 1967 Ford J-Car, which would become part of Mattel's first line of cars. **Next pages:** An original advertisement for the Sweet Sixteen and all the cars in their bright, rad, rodded, rolling glory.

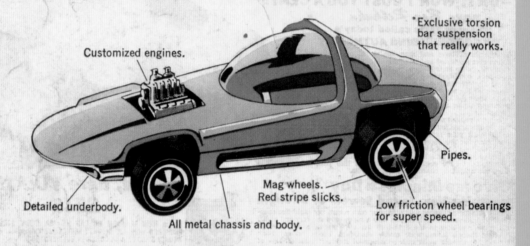

Silhouette

Custom Volkswagen

Custom Camaro

Deora

Custom Firebird

Custom Barracuda

Ford J-Car

Custom Fleetside

Beatnik Bandit

Custom Eldorado

Hot Heap

Custom Mustang

Python

Custom Corvette

Custom T-Bird

Custom Cougar

CUSTOM CULTURE'S WILD RIDES

Hot Wheels were not ahead of their time. They were squarely on time, tapping an interest in fast cars and customizing that coursed through the airwaves, rumbled over streets, and splashed across magazine spreads and TV screens. There was a creativity and authenticity to the racing scene that the Mattel team saw the toy market was ready to match.

One of the hottest bands in the early '60s glorified surfing, girls, and fast cars. Beach Boys' lyrics bragged, "We always take my car 'cause it's never been beat" ("I Get Around"), "Tach it up, tach it up/Buddy gonna shut you down" ("Shut Down"), and "Nothing can catch her, nothing can touch my 4-0-9" ("409"). Even more apt for a Handler-led company was "Little Deuce Coupe," the very car Ruth had been driving (an enclosed '32 Ford) the first time she noticed her future husband, Elliot, on a Denver street.

Hot-rod culture had evolved on California's dry lake beds, where drivers found higher speeds by trimming weight. They removed hoods and fenders, shortened exhaust systems, fitted high-performance components, and added wider tires for better grip. Chroming newly exposed engine parts gave them a gleaming audacity, while pinstriping and custom paint could lend a unique finishing touch.

After World War II, another race—to space—was also underway between the United States and the Soviet Union. Scientific and artistic renderings of advanced flight technology pushed into popular culture, where the imagery was absorbed by automotive stylists and incorporated into their designs. Major manufacturers built numerous show cars in the 1950s with space and aircraft styling. GM's Firebird prototypes from 1953 to 1959 looked like rockets or jets with road wheels. Like Lincoln's Futura of 1955, they featured cockpit-style rounded or bubble windscreens. Custom builders drew on hot-rod and futuristic influences, and so did Hot Wheels' designers when speed surfaced as the key theme for the small-cars project.

Ed "Big Daddy" Roth was a provocative figure on the hot-rod scene. He was an artist and car builder known for his rebellious rodent, Rat Fink, a bulging-eyed, seedy, and depraved-looking counterpoint to Disney's pure-hearted, white-gloved mouse. Roth sold Rat Fink T-shirts to make money for car projects, including the retro-modern Beatnik Bandit. For Bandit, Roth cut down an Oldsmobile chassis

Top: The hot-rod vibe was in the air—literally in the radio waves, from the Beach Boys' "Little Deuce Coupe"—and Mattel's designers tuned in. **Middle:** Ed "Big Daddy" Roth at work in his garage. His creations helped set the tone of Hot Wheels custom machines for decades to follow. **Bottom:** Roth built the car dubbed Druid Princess for TV's *The Addams Family*, but the show was canceled before the car could appear.

and fitted a hand-built fiberglass body, leaving the blown V-8 to tower, exposed, in front of the bubble-top canopy. *Rod & Custom* magazine ran the car in June 1960. Roth sketched monster-driven hot rods igniting the pavement with burning rubber and blazing exhausts.

Creatures and customs also combined on television in *The Munsters*, which debuted in 1964. The show's Munster Koach and Drag-u-la were built at Barris Kustom, which would also transform the Lincoln Futura into the Batmobile for the 1966 *Batman* movie and TV show. In time, the Batmobile would enter the Hot Wheels lineup.

The Sweet Sixteen's Silhouette and Python were styled after full-size customs by Cushenberry Custom Shop. The founder, Bill Cushenberry, had started his own auto-body business in Wichita, Kansas, when he was just nineteen years old. His hometown already had a hotshot builder, Darryl Starbird, turning out performance art from his Star Kustom Shop, prompting Cushenberry to relocate to Monterey, California. He built an eye-catching '40 Ford called El Matador that put his name on enthusiasts' tongues.

For the original, full-size Silhouette, Cushenberry shortened a Buick chassis and fitted an open-wheel, pointy-nose body, hand-crafted in steel. He used a Buick V-8 to start but swapped in a 427 Ford when the car was invited to participate in the Ford Custom Car Caravan, a touring showcase of top builders' work. As had Roth on Beatnik Bandit, Cushenberry crowned Silhouette with a bubble top, similar to the one on the Jetsons' spacecraft in the family cartoon, which began about the same time in 1962.

The full-size car mimicked by Python first took shape in *Car Craft* magazine as Dream Rod, an unusual, asymmetric design drawn by its staff. The sketch impressed car-show promoter Bob Larivee. After viewing the Silhouette at the 1963 Grand National Roadster Show, Larivee hired Cushenberry to build a real car based on the Dream Rod. The customizer blended chassis, body, and engine parts from a Jowett Jupiter, Volkswagen, Pontiac, Corvair, Studebaker, Mercury, Lincoln, Ford, and a Borgward Isabella Sedan to fashion the car. In 1966 it was restyled as the Tiger Shark, with front fenders arched over the wheel wells, a hood scoop, and other modifications. Dean Jeffries, a top builder in his own right, did the Hot Wheels design for Python (née Cheetah) based on the Tiger Shark version of the Dream Rod, adding an exposed, chromed engine.

By embracing the custom-car scene, models such as Silhouette, Beatnik Bandit, and Python set the stage for generations of unrestrained Hot Wheels designs to accompany high-performance, production-based models.

Top: Bill Cushenberry's Silhouette inspired a car in the Sweet Sixteen, using the same aviation-style acrylic for its canopy that Elliot Handler worked with at art school. **Middle:** The same material gave the Lincoln Futura its distinctive windscreen, later peered through by the caped crusaders. **Bottom:** George Barris's shop modified the body of the Futura for a superhero feel.

HOT WHEELS DESIGN

To launch his toy car idea, Elliot Handler wanted people trained in automobile design. At first, it was a correlation clearer to him than to them, but over the decades many designers have come to see that Mattel can offer at least as much as Detroit—and perhaps more.

Harry Bradley took the job mostly so he could move to California. Larry Wood did so because he needed work. Phil Riehlman first came to Mattel to assist with an overflow of work during the time the company was transitioning to 3-D modeling.

In time, all of Mattel's designers come to appreciate the remarkable creativity they can apply working on Hot Wheels. The miniature vehicles are made in huge numbers, they have extraordinary variety, and they borrow from road-going machines and inspire them too. Real autos push Hot Wheels, and Hot Wheels push real vehicles right back.

Larry Wood has had a huge influence on the brand. He started in September 1969, shortly after the Sweet Sixteen launched, and continued to design and innovate for the next forty years. Like Bradley, he had been in Detroit, working for Ford from 1965 to 1967. He preferred the vibe in California, though, where he had studied at Art Center School of Design in Los Angeles. He hitchhiked back without a job and found contract work at the Lockheed Corporation, designing plane interiors. But Lockheed was going through layoffs and did not seem like a long-term prospect.

The Hot Wheels opportunity was pure happenstance. Wood went to a party, where he spoke to Howard Rees, with whom he had worked at Ford. Rees was leaving a job, and Wood was looking. Rees put in a good word with his employer, Mattel. The connection got Wood an interview with Elliot Handler. Wood had the chops Elliot was seeking.

Above: Designer Larry Wood created the tow truck Ramblin' Wrecker. He added Larry's 24 HR. TOWING on the side. He also put his own phone number on the original drawing, which was never removed in production—a mistake he learned of when a boy dialed it at Christmas to talk about the toy. This 2009 reissue omits the phone number.

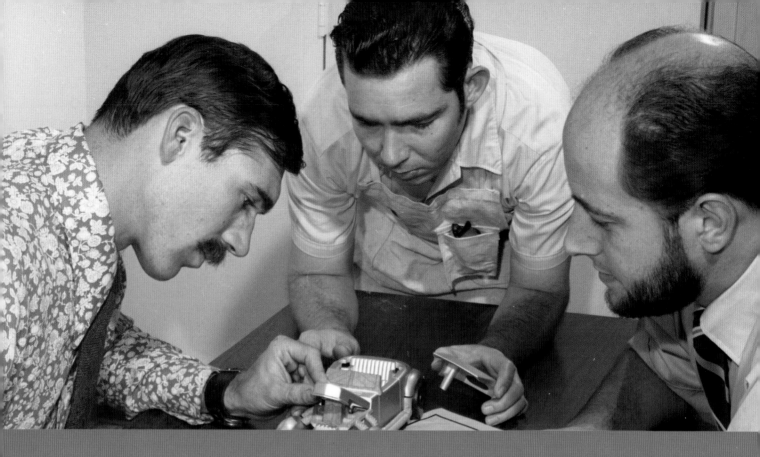

AT THE JUNCTION OF WORK AND PLAY

Wood didn't mention that he hadn't played with toy cars as a kid. He was more about cowboy games with toy guns. His fixation with cars arose from a coincidence of geography. His family's home sat along the main road to a Connecticut beach. As a teenager, Wood took an interest in the alluring machines rolling past with rumbling engines, flashy chrome, and cool operators not much older than himself. Cap-gun play had nothing on cruising. He bought his own car and modified it using *Hot Rod* magazine for reference.

Wood imagined that the Mattel job would be temporary—something to survive on until the next thing came along. The work changed his view, and Wood made a huge impression on Hot Wheels. He finished up a couple of designs Rees had begun, including Noodle Head, and over the ensuing four decades went on to contribute more of his own designs than he can track.

As the economy ebbed and flowed, there were times when Wood was the sole designer, penning away in collaboration with an engineer.

Wood closely followed the earliest designers, such as Bradley and Ira Gilford, and overlapped with many who came later, including Riehlman. And it wasn't lack of fun or shortage of ideas that led Wood to retire. Mostly, it was a change in approach. Wood likes to sketch, to capture flights of fancy by hand, on drafting paper. He decided to leave when the primary approach switched to digital creation. He doesn't deplore that method—he admires the beautiful imagery it can produce. It just isn't his preferred way to conceptualize. That being the case, he chose to continue working with Mattel as a consultant where he could still lend his considerable talent to the process without having to perfect a new skill he didn't feel necessary.

Above: Larry Wood examines an unpainted model of the Classic Cord, with two Mattel engineers, before the Hot Wheels' version was released in 1971.

Phil Riehlman also has a long tenure at Mattel, where he designs track sets and vehicles, including many models beloved by collectors. He's inspired by the ability to design the whole car and carry it through to a completed miniature ready for consumers. This is not how it happens at auto manufacturers. "Most kids want to design the next performance car," he said, like "a muscle car or exotic." Yet those desirable jobs are rare. A young designer is more likely to start working on something mundane, such as door handles or badging, and may never style a Corvette or Lamborghini.

With Hot Wheels, performance runs through the heart of the product line. Every vehicle designed for use with the play sets must perform up to expectations. Not all lines are built for flat-out speed, however. Mattel recognizes that some kids are more interested in vehicles styled after characters from TV or movies. Their play may be more tailored to bad guys, good guys, chases, and heroics than racing for first place.

Also, designers must operate within some boundaries for practicality and cost. Mattel is not going to retool a fresh wheel size for every new model, for example. Rather, designers will take the line's available wheel sizes into consideration from the start, as well as through the steps of modeling the vehicle from initial to final scale.

When Wood began with Mattel, four-up and three-up models (four times and three times larger than ¹⁄₆₄) would be created in wood or clay and reviewed in physical form. For ¹⁄₆₄ size, the actual production dimensions of certain details, such as a gas-filler panel or door handle, have to be exaggerated so they're not indistinguishably small. Viewed three-up or four-up, that exaggeration looks clunky. Today, the bigger versions of the designs are viewed on a screen as 3-D images, and no physical model is produced other than at ¹⁄₆₄.

Computer modeling has greatly accelerated the production timeline. The layout drawings the designers produce from their sketches can be translated much more quickly to a 3-D computer model than to a physical model carved from wood or shaped in clay. Likewise, the scale-down process is very swift. Riehlman says he can get 3-D files for one of his designs in the morning and be looking

Above: The Ira Gilford–designed *Fire Chief Cruiser* from 1970, beside its 4x larger handmade precursor in epoxy. The 1969 *Custom Police Cruiser* uses the same casting with different paint.

at a 1/64-scale digital physical model by lunchtime on the same day. In earlier times, it could take a week to get a model based on drawings. Not all designers work digitally though. Riehlman still likes to sketch by hand on paper initially and then do the coloring later on the computer.

Working with toy cars of any scale is rewarding, and Mattel employees enjoy the experience of a work environment that emphasizes fun. Although work volume is high and fast-paced, there are unusual benefits.

When Wood began at Mattel, he found it different than any other company he had been at. There was a true sense of family. He and colleagues would take camping trips into the desert to ride motorcycles and experience the varied California landscape. The atmosphere at their desks, while generally focused and professional, could also be playful. Wood and colleagues had a gap between their office walls and a line of windows, down which they ran a toy train. Sometimes they would send notes back and forth. Once a colleague sent a train car to Wood carrying a dollop of rubber cement that was on fire, which Wood promptly extinguished.

Riehlman, a recurring guest at Hot Wheels conventions, is often asked which of his many designs is his favorite. He always responds, "the next one," because investing each new creation with his full creativity is part of the job—its requirement and reward. Even standard production vehicles that may seem ordinary can present an enticing challenge to find the enhancements that make them radical. Riehlman's hopped-up vans and delivery vehicles, such as the VW Drag Bus and Drag Dairy, are popular examples. Working for the auto manufacturers, he would have had nowhere near the number of different design opportunities presented by Mattel.

Riehlman is not alone in his opinion of working for a company that makes play out of work. Lots of innovative thinkers who went to automotive design school find a satisfying home at Mattel, making vehicles of all sorts and capabilities. Their goal with their education was to make real cars, but "real" is a matter of perspective. The children and collectors that gleefully buy their designs consider these toy cars as real as any.

Above: Gilford's *Torero* from 1969, beside a painted resin version, also at 1:64 scale. The epoxy mock-up is fitted with a set of worn wheels. **Next page:** (left) Larry Wood, Hot Wheels designer from 1969 to 2009. (right) Larry Wood concept sketches.

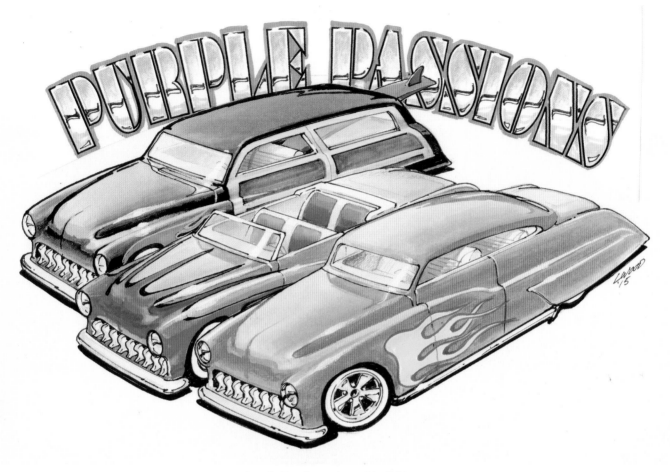

Purple Passion, released in 1990.

Ramblin' Wrecker, released in 1975.

Purple Passion and Bone Shaker,
released in 1990 and 2006, respectively.

Pass'n Gasser, released in 2008.

Bone Shaker, released in 2006.

Wood's take on Gilford's Twin Mill.

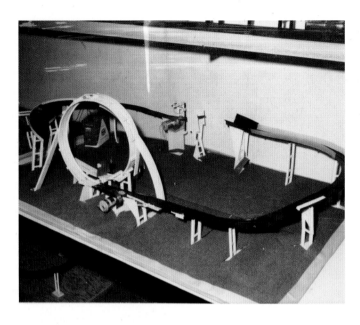

TRACK STARS AND STUNT CARS

Early in the design process, Fred Adickes wanted to study the developmental cars rolling under gravity power. He entered a hardware store on his way home from Mattel and found a length of garage door weather stripping that was flat with raised edges. The next day, he brought it to work with a C-clamp and affixed it to a shelf, pointing the other end out his office door. He sent a demo car zipping into the hall. Elliot and Jack Ryan soon arrived to admire the setup, and the track sets were born. This first track was just the beginning of what would come.

The Handlers liked to build on success by supplementing toy lines to increase sales and sustain buyer interest. With their brisk speed, Hot Wheels had play value beyond what wood, linoleum, or concrete floors could offer. Here was a toy that deserved its own venue. Mattel turned its developers loose to create accessories that would showcase the cars' performance. By Toy Fair 1968, an array of tracks and trestles with gravity-defying loops and ramps proved that Hot Wheels could out-stunt any competitor on the market.

Engineering claimed the cars' scaled speed surpassed two hundred miles per hour. These fast cars had the momentum to perform jumps and inverted moves that would crash more slothful toys. High speeds also sent a vehicle off the track more easily, placing some limits

on all-out haste. Mattel's accessory lineup provided purpose-built drag strip, circuit racing, and stunt driving environments designed to meet the desire for fast cars while compensating for the challenges of moving at excessive speeds.

Race kits were a natural for the industry's fastest miniature cars, and Mattel offered four versions the first year its Hot Wheels line was on the market. The Strip Action Set was the simplest of the bunch, essentially a standardized production of Adickes's hardware-store creation. Instead of weather stripping, it featured the soon-to-be signature bright orange extruded plastic track in two-foot lengths, joined via underside tongue-in-groove connectors. A plastic C-clamp, molded with track and accessory fittings, was used to attach the plastic roadway to a raised surface—such as a table or chair. The clamp allowed children to start their cars from a point as high as the physics of plastic allowed, providing even more boost to their racers as they sped down the track.

Left: Until the familiar base piece was developed for production, designers did what they could to hold track in a loop—like this flying-buttress approach for their 1967 track prototype.

SECONDS !

The Drag Race Action Set was the competition version of the race kit, with *two* clamp-mounted starting gates that held competing cars. A single button released the pair, which sped toward a finish gate on the ground below. The winner tripped a checkered flag before both lanes funneled into one in what Mattel called the elimination lane. In a clear win, the "eliminated" car fell in behind first place, while in tight races, both cars could be jettisoned by the resulting collision.

The Stunt Action Set was a single-lane kit, with a start-where-you-dare clamp, a loop, pair of ramps, and a stomach-pitching trestle for a quick up-down. Its jumps made a true break in the circuit and could be set any distance apart, while the loop required high entry speed to keep a car on track. Together, the ramps and loop-the-loop separated quick-sprint Hot Wheels vehicles from their slower rivals. Mattel's cars soared in an arcing flash, while other makes plopped over to await a toy tow truck.

Curves were another trial for these rolling rockets, and cars that entered a turn too hot would sail wide and

car and extra track available separately

Hot Wheels
FASTEST METAL CARS IN THE WORLD!

DAREDEVIL LOOP
ACCESSORY PAK
BY MATTEL

*360° DRIVE-IN
LOOP-THE-LOOP*

**TO BE USED
ONLY WITH
HOT WHEELS
ACTION SETS
& POPUP
PLAY SETS!**

Above and right: Mattel hired California freelance artist Otto Kuhni to provide engaging illustrations that could be used on packaging and promotional materials. Kuhni's bright colors and sense of motion were a perfect complement to the speedy die-casts.

tumble. The Toy Fair team encountered such issues at its debut show. Mattel could have contained Hot Wheels with enclosed corners, like a modern waterslide's, but that was counterproductive. The racers' ability to fly off the track was proof of their swiftness in a market where competitors' models mostly ground to a halt.

The Hot Curves Race Action Set tested the twists by bending a pair of cars through 90- and 180-degree banked curves. Six trestles could be used to raise the curves on one or both lanes where elevated turns further raised the stakes on overzealous speed. As with the drag set, a finish gate dropped a checkered flag for the winner.

Different track setups could affect the outcome, as heavier models accelerated more quickly against friction on the inclined start, but lighter cars rolled faster on the flat. Adroitness through curves, ramps, and loops could also separate the best from the rest.

Another selling point for Hot Wheels was their pocket size, which carried through to their accessories as well. They were unobtrusive in homes where space is limited, and tracks disassembled for easy stowage in a cabinet or closet or under the bed.

Mattel continued this space efficiency with a line of pop-up kits to round out the play atmosphere. The original kits unfolded into a service station, speed shop, house with carport, speedway race set, and a carrying case for a dozen cars combined with a grandstand crowded with speed freaks. Made with brightly colored graphics on vinyl over cardboard, each kit came with one or two cars. Because of the frequent use Hot Wheels typically got and the five decades that have passed, most of the early kits show wear, distortion, or other damage. Kits in new condition are rare.

Top: Photos of real kids from a 1967 and 1969 catalog, enjoying the actual toys.
Bottom: This 1968 Mattel ad showed any kid or parent what the product would look like in their own living room.

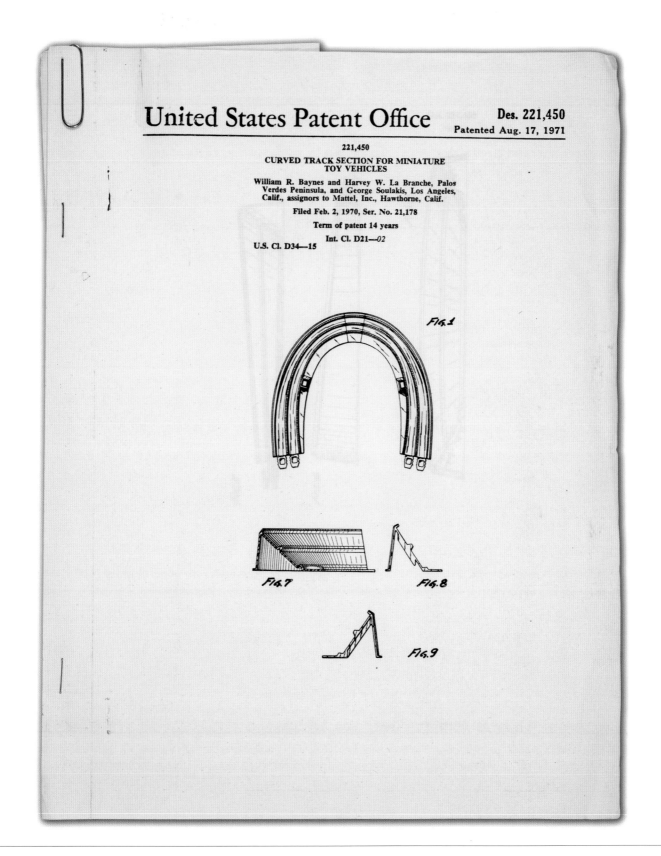

United States Patent Office

Des. 221,450
Patented Aug. 17, 1971

221,450

CURVED TRACK SECTION FOR MINIATURE TOY VEHICLES

William R. Baynes and Harvey W. La Branche, Palos Verdes Peninsula, and George Soulakis, Los Angeles, Calif., assignors to Mattel, Inc., Hawthorne, Calif.

Filed Feb. 2, 1970, Ser. No. 21,178

Term of patent 14 years

Int. Cl. D21—02

U.S. Cl. D34—15

Fig. 1

Fig. 7

Fig. 8

Fig. 9

Above: Copy of a U.S. patent for a curved track section of Hot Wheels track, 1971. In the ravenous toy market, protecting intellectual property is critical. The date on a box or the underside of a car is often earlier than the year of production because that's when rights were secured—before the product left Mattel's Hawthorne, CA, headquarters.

BACKIN' THE BEASTS

Racing is like platelets. It's in the blood. If your DNA contains the "racer" sequence, you're going to the track as sure as you have brown eyes or attached earlobes. The trick is that traits such as curly hair and quick reflexes are free, but racing isn't. Car culture comes with unrelenting expenses, on top of food and bills for the homes that drivers maintain but seldom see.

Don "the Snake" Prudhomme and Tom "the Mongoose" McEwen were born drag racers, devoting mind, body, and soul to devouring a quarter mile faster than any challenger on any strip. Their passion consumed fuel and oxygen and cash. Injected into that combustive environment, sponsorship dollars could provide more speed, more wins, safer cars, and saner lives.

Mattel had money, plus an outstanding new toy line called Hot Wheels. The Snake and the Mongoose offered heart, major talent, a compelling rivalry, and access to present and future race fans, including legions of kids. McEwen connected these elements in a sponsorship deal that changed racing, opening it to big-time, nonautomotive patrons. Mattel would later enter into additional partnerships, including NASCAR, Indycar, NHRA/Jon Force, Moto GP (Jorge Lorenzo), and Felipe Massa (F1).

Like Mattel and much of cool-car culture, the Snake-Mongoose rivalry was born in Southern California. The roof Don Prudhomme was raised under was paid for by his father's auto-body shop. Young Don was sanding cars before he could drive—more for need of cash than love of body repair. His dream was four-wheeled and V-8–powered, inspired by the first hot rod he saw as a boy, his cousin Harold's '32 roadster street racer cradling a DeSoto Hemi engine.

Prudhomme's fixation put him in the company of other men who obsessed over fast machines. He bought

Top left: Don Prudhomme wears a smile here, but at the wheel he was one of the fiercest, most focused competitors on the strip. **Top right:** Tom McEwen was a top driver who showed up to win. **Bottom right:** Hot Wheels capitalized on the Snake-Mongoose rivalry with their 1970 drag race set.

MONGOOSE AND SNAKE

a road car himself and eventually joined a car club called the Road Kings. They shared tools, parts, knowledge, and seat time, ultimately getting the man who would become the Snake into the drag-racing scene.

Tommy Ivo was a pivotal member-friend. In addition to driving, Ivo was a working actor with money and name recognition. He invited Prudhomme to join him on a national drag-race tour of tracks that would pay Ivo an appearance fee. For Prudhomme, it was "Drag Race College." He ran gofer duty while sponging up the critical knowledge all around him—how to read a track, set up a car, tune injectors, and adjust the clutch. He studied how Ivo drove the varied strips and how he booked appearances, handled promoters, and got publicity. From the time Prudhomme returned from that journey in 1959, he treated racing seriously. It's where his mind was and where he was determined his future would be.

Fortunately, his reflexes and determination suited his high-speed, low elapsed-time (ET) goals. By 1962, at just twenty years old, he beat a field of the best Top Fuel drivers in the country to win the U.S. Fuel & Gas Championships in Bakersfield, California. A phenomenal car then came his way, owned by Tommy Greer and rebuilt, after its engine blew, by Kent Fuller and Wayne Ewing, with a new engine by Keith Black. At the controls of the Greer, Black, and Prudhomme dragster, Don became an elite driver. A crew member named Joel Purcell dubbed him "the Snake"—a predator to strike at all rivals.

Tom McEwen was the son of a test pilot who died in a crash before Tom was two years old. His mother had moved him and his little brother from Florida to California, where his love of speed took hold. At fifteen, Tom sneaked his mom's Oldsmobile to a Santa Ana drag strip and flatfooted a couple quarter miles. He

Above: This angle closely approximates Prudhomme's car in a rearview mirror on the rival lane.

then bought the first '55 Chevy V-8 in Long Beach, fitted a supercharger, and had some success before switching to a blown Hemi–powered Fiat altered-coupe with partner Bud Rasner. When that engine exploded at Lions Drag Strip, track manager Mickey Thompson came over and said, "Kid, if you want to do real racing, you should get yourself a dragster."

McEwen was hired by hall-of-fame crew chief Gene Adams to drive the Albertson Olds, a supercharged dragster in which Leonard Harris had won the 1960 National Hot Rod Association (NHRA) Nationals in Detroit. McEwen replaced Harris, who had been killed test-driving another car. When McEwen found his form, he began winning too.

He and Prudhomme crossed paths, off the strip and on. While Prudhomme was quieter, more intense, laser-focused on tuning, and driving to win, McEwen was joking, conversational, and alert to the broader scene. Their opposite personalities and comparable skills made for a natural rivalry—the talkative, fun-loving McEwen versus the guarded, fierce Prudhomme. McEwen could lose with a self-effacing quip; Prudhomme would charge his opponent's pit, shouting, swinging, and asserting foul play.

At Pomona, California, McEwen says he "cheated the lights" and beat his rival in the nearly invincible Greer Black dragster. Ed Donovan, owner of McEwen's car at the time, told him that he had just beaten the Snake, and therefore McEwen should be "the Mongoose." The business-savvy McEwen ran with it, getting an artist to paint the meanest, ugliest caricature of the animal possible on his helmet. He showed it to Prudhomme and said, "Let's push this thing." Prudhomme nodded and got his lid adorned with a nasty serpent. They held Snake-versus-Mongoose match races at Long Beach, where the crowds fell in fervently behind their favorite beast.

Long-view McEwen sensed the rivalry's value beyond the drag strip. He felt it might interest the local maker of toy cars and race sets. Jerry Frye was Mattel's director of product planning, reviewing three thousand proposals a year—99 percent of which the company rejected. McEwen brought him the Snake-Mongoose pitch, and Frye tuned in. After Mattel met Prudhomme, it was a done deal.

Designer Larry Wood set to work at once on a pair of Hot Wheels funny cars in honor of the furry and scaly rivals. Funny cars feature stock-looking bodies hinged to tubular race chassis, and the Snake and Mongoose

Above: Along with the awesome roar of McEwan's floored V-8 drag engine, billowing tire smoke was an audience thriller.

used theirs to maximum effect, igniting the crowds with long, smoky burnouts—done in theory to warm the tires—exaggerated to half-track length for adrenaline and show. Although Mattel later introduced dragsters—Prudhomme's preferred ride—it was the funny cars that gave the rivals a national following, particularly with kids.

The Snake and the Mongoose toured nationally. Before they hit each town, Mattel would coordinate with a local shopping mall to set up a large competition Hot Wheels track, where kids would come and race their cars and meet their heroes. Youngsters loved it, stores loved it, tracks loved it, and Prudhomme and McEwen loved it too, especially meeting and interacting with youthful fans.

The pair's first sponsored funny cars appeared in 1970, with McEwen under a red fiberglass Plymouth Duster body and Prudhomme a yellow Barracuda. Mattel stayed on as a major sponsor until 1973, then went to associate sponsor, giving the drivers a royalty on the toys bearing their monikers to this day.

That era marked an impassioned rivalry, with the Snake taking more races overall but the Mongoose winning some of the biggest ones. Some fans were so devoted, they'd get tattoos of their chosen beast. At

one race, two shirtless brothers walked up to the pro drivers while they were talking to fans. One kid had the Mongoose inked on his chest, the other the Snake. Each one had also had an open circle tattooed on his arm. They asked their chosen driver to sign in the circle, which McEwen and Prudhomme did. The siblings then went immediately to the tattoo shop to have the signatures inked in permanently. Even now, multigenerational families will approach the drag racers with worn-out Snake and Mongoose Hot Wheels and faded tattoos to express their thanks for providing them with such fun and excitement.

And don't ask if the drivers ever decided the winner in advance. No way! As Prudhomme said, "I hate losing so much that if I would have let Tom win a race, I couldn't have looked at myself in the mirror." McEwen added that racing was a job, and he was there to earn money, not just put on a show. The difference was that McEwen wanted to win when it mattered. He wouldn't thrash his engine all-out if he had already qualified. Prudhomme would, though; he wanted to win every single time he lined up against anyone, anywhere, for any reason. That's the Snake and the Mongoose.

Top left: Prudhomme and McEwen earned their strong reputations racing dragsters, rather than funny cars. **Top and bottom right:** When Mattel came aboard, its customers were more familiar with the road-car look featured in this Hot Wheels ad.

OTHER DIMENSIONS:
2-D TO 3-D

No matter how many words a picture tells, the story can never be as complete as looking at the actual subject. Two dimensions cannot perfectly mimic three. A car show is an easy place to observe this phenomenon. You find a sightline across the nose of a Porsche or Jaguar that captures its provocative curves. When you frame it up in your camera, however, the magic disappears. It looks less voluptuous, less inviting, less "real."

The extra pizzazz evoked by the actual vehicle arises from binocular disparity—the slight discrepancy between the car as viewed by your left eye and your right eye. When flattened to a static image on a screen, however, there is no depth to perceive. Each eye can see all the lines and all the surface area comprising the picture. Even an image presenting cues for three dimensions, such as light highlights and linear perspective, still looks flat.

Elliot and his designers were aware of the distinctions between drawn and real objects. Throughout automotive history, car builders have relied on three-dimensional modeling to sight-test their designs, to better gauge the impression that the actual vehicle will create. While modern designers have access to 3-D imaging programs, major manufacturers still will not approve a car for production without first viewing it in accurate, model form. Too much money depends on a design's market success

to infer real-world appeal based on a two-dimensional presentation, even one that simulates depth.

The first tangible effort to create a new Hot Wheels car typically occurs on a sketchpad—hard copy initially and now with an option of sketching digitally. Here, designers resolve their amorphous inspirations into lines and proportions that can be preserved, studied, modified, and reviewed by colleagues. Elliot had his designers put their sketches where he could see them as he walked around the design floor.

In addition to the complete vehicle body, designers envision the component parts that must be individually cast and assembled to make the whole. They also consider particular styling highlights to imbue the vehicle with the desired look and aura.

Although overall accuracy and precision are important, not every detail present on a full-size automobile translates well to a miniature. Certain features such as keyholes, gas-filler panels, side mirrors, or radio antennae are too small to replicate practically or in a way that benefits looks and performance. The modeling process provides opportunity to explore fine details from appearance, function, and manufacturing perspectives.

Over its history, Mattel has used various materials and scales to shape its designs in three dimensions. A common early size was the "four-up" model. This was

Above: These images are two dimensional, with height and width but no depth. The sketch (left) simulates depth with shading. The photograph (right) of the Python resin prototype captures light, as reflected by the three-dimensional contours. It gives us a clearer sense of the car's surface but provides no better understanding of what is unseen.

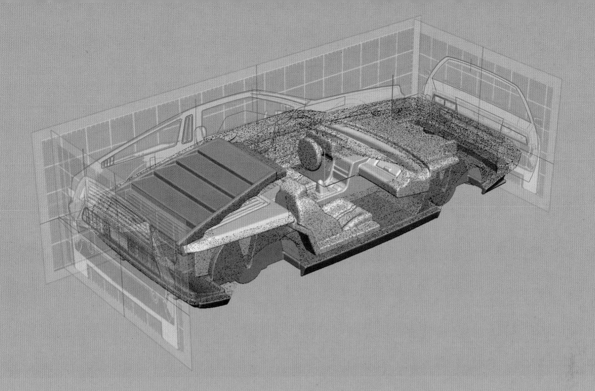

at 1/16 scale, or four times larger than the finished 1/64 version. Vehicles at this size might be carved out of wood or made from epoxy. Three-up models were three times production size. When shaped, the model was taken to the designer for review and potential revision.

When the larger-size model was approved, scale would be further reduced. Some versions might be made in clear or translucent plastic, to see how the components fit together. Others would be painted to create a more accurate impression of what a production version would look like.

Hot Wheels based on existing automobiles benefit from the work already done. Photographers can capture the vehicle from all angles, and design personnel can take precise measurements. This information can then be translated by Mattel engineers into mechanical drawings. In the computer-aided design era, the data are converted to surface files, which can be used along with the photographs to generate a 3-D digital image of the car. Often, auto manufacturers will share their CAD files with Mattel to facilitate the process. From here, as with the pre-CAD era, the detailed data is used to make a scale model, which is then reviewed and refined as necessary. A pattern is then made and approved, from which the steel die used to cast the production body is cut.

Mattel's modern process involves hand-drawn or digital sketches, then a digital solid model, a digital tooling model, an engineering pilot, a final engineering pilot, and a production pilot. At each point, the product is carefully reviewed and approved before it can move on to the next stage.

Occasionally—despite all the preproduction planning, engineering, and review—a Hot Wheels model would be fully completed in paint and detail, ready for market in appearance, yet it would fail the play test. The Beach Bomb is the classic example. Based on a VW bus, with two surfboards protruding out the rear window, it was finely detailed and authentic and cool. On looks alone, it had to be a marketing favorite. Beach Bomb was chill while still. It would look fantastic behind plastic.

But it was whack on the track. The narrow body barely engaged the Super-Charger's spinning foam accelerator wheels—which was just as well, because the top-heavy van went wheels up at the first turn. Surely some bragging on the way home from the toy store would have been silenced had the new Beach Bombs gone cartwheeling across the living room floor.

Ultimately, though, it turned out well. Mattel reworked the design, and time fixed the rest, as the low-production Beach Bomb has become one of the most collectible Hot Wheels ever produced.

Above: The 3-D rendering here provides more information and conveys a sense of the whole—including color, shading, graining, and "flattened" views of the front, side, and rear. Nothing flat or on a screen can provide a true a sense of the finished Hot Wheels as a sculpted model—though a 3-D image, where it can be rotated, is close.

HOT WHEELS SCULPTING

Manson Cheung photographs cars. He doesn't care how many horses are on tap or who manufactured it, nor is he concerned with what it costs. His eyes are drawn to shapes and expressive lines. When he's moved by the way a vehicle's surfaces flow together and catch the light, he takes a picture. Then he uses these snaps as inspiration for his work as a sculptor for Hot Wheels.

In practice, that career has changed drastically. Early modelers worked with even-grained wood, shaping and paring by hand with steel chisels and other carving tools. They took big cuts early on, turning to finer, more precise instruments and movements as they whittled their project toward final dimensions, revealing the shape only they saw hidden within.

The medium has evolved from wooden blocks to digital clay, yet the modern sculpting process is much the same. Today's modelers have replaced their carving tools with a joystick-style controller driven by software that allows the designer to slice through space with the same subtle paring motions used by master crafters of old. The process eliminates waste, reduces raw materials costs, and accelerates production. A modeler can mirror a sculpted side to replace the uncarved side, saving substantial effort. And the finished shape is data that can be 3-D printed for review by the designer.

This haptic technology mimics the feel of real-world sculpting. Depending on the fineness or coarseness of the digital clay selected, the haptic controller provides more or less resistance to its manipulation. When the sculptor moves the virtual tool off the onscreen clay, the resistance drops to near zero—like a chisel passed through air. When tool and object touch onscreen, the controller simulates resistance equal to a real tool-point meeting actual clay.

Above: Short Order, designed by Howard Rees, was released in 1971 in die-cast form. This example in Spectraflame Light Green sits next to its 4x wood mock-up, in 1970.

A MATTER OF PERSPECTIVE

The finer the digital clay, the more information it provides, showing a 3-D surface in sharp detail in the same way more dots per inch (dpi) provide higher resolution in a printed image. A model sculpted with fine virtual clay can be zoomed into and viewed with greater clarity. A 3-D model printed from it will be smoother and more precise.

Cheung is one of about twenty modelers in Mattel's Sculpting Group, which does all the modeling for the company and its subdivisions. His work focuses overwhelmingly on Hot Wheels. He can appreciate the differences and similarities between real and digital paring because he has worked with both methods. Beginning in 2003, he hand-sculpted several Hot Wheels designs from RenShape, a polyurethane foam, and from wax. The transition to digital was easy because of the similarity in feel.

Reduced sculpting times in the digital era have helped Mattel produce many more new Hot Wheels designs annually—about 150 now, compared to as few as twelve to sixteen in the early years. Since 2007 Cheung has sculpted about six hundred of the vehicles digitally. It takes him about twenty to forty hours to sculpt a design from scratch.

When a vehicle is current and production-based, Mattel often gets digital files from the automobile manufacturer. The modeler can load those, then make changes. Because the toy's wheel sizes are predetermined, for example, the real version's wheel arches typically must be adjusted. Other details, like shut lines, may also be resized so that they translate well at $1/64$ scale.

With an original Mattel car design, the process is different. The designer first captures it in a sketch, either by hand on paper, or digitally, such as with a stylus and screen. Sometimes, control drawings—layout drawings that

Above: Digital imagery allows multiple parts to be studied individually as seen in this layered view of the die-cast elements. **Next page:** Designers come to love the creative freedom that Hot Wheels permits as seen in these concept sketches.

Twin Mill, released in 1969. Illustration by Ira Gilford.

Lotus Turbine, released in 1969. Illustration by Ira Gilford.

Splittin' Image, released in 1969. Illustration by Ira Gilford.

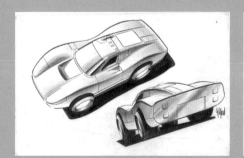

Ford Mark IV, released in 1969.
Illustration by Ira Gilford.

Chaparral 2G, released in 1969.
Illustration by Ira Gilford.

Turbofire, released in 1969.
Illustration by Ira Gilford.

Peepin' Bomb, released in 1970. Illustration by Howard Rees.

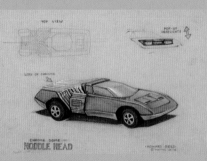

Cockney Cab, released in 1971.
Illustration by Howard Rees.

Short Order, released in 1971.
Illustration by Howard Rees.

Noodle Head, released in 1971.
Illustration by Howard Rees.

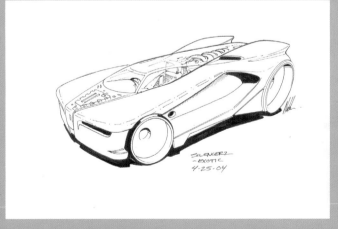

Spine Buster, released in 2005. Illustration by Nathan Proch.

Anthracite, released in 2005. Illustration by Nathan Proch.

Back to the Future - Time Machine

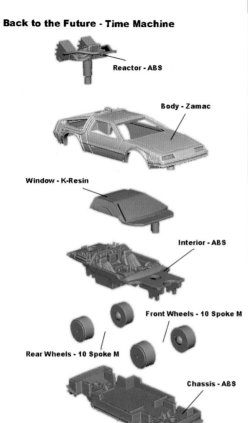

Reactor - ABS

Body - Zamac

Window - K-Resin

Interior - ABS

Front Wheels - 10 Spoke M

Rear Wheels - 10 Spoke M

Chassis - ABS

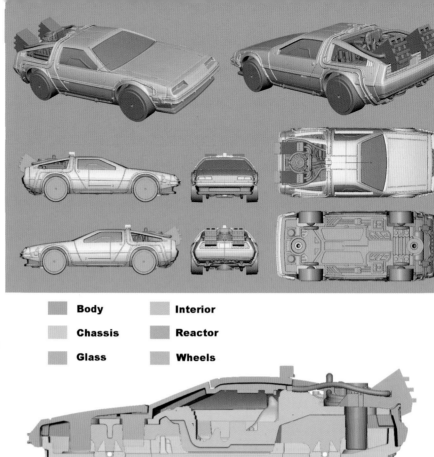

■ Body		■ Interior	
■ Chassis		■ Reactor	
■ Glass		■ Wheels	

Above: Manson Cheung designed the DeLorean-based *Back to the Future* Time Machine, which utilized his interests in digital sculpting, movies, and the automobile.
Bottom: The *Back to the Future* car in hover mode, with its clear base.

show the vehicle from many angles—are provided. The modeler uses these references to create an accurate digital sculpture, which is then 3-D printed for designer review.

On top of all of his sculpting, Cheung has also designed several dozen Hot Wheels. Many of these have been entertainment cars, which originate from pop culture rather than automotive impulses. A vehicle like that can stymie the car fanatics in Design Group. When it does, a designer might stroll down to Sculpting, tell Cheung the assignment, and say, "I don't get it." Usually that's an invitation—a gauntlet Cheung snatches up with an enthusiastic "Dude, I get it! I'm on it!"

While most Hot Wheels design staff members have degrees in transportation design, Cheung has a toy design degree from Otis College of Art and Design. He's also a movie and TV buff who welcomes the opportunity to apply that interest to his work. He digs into his own references, conducts research, and reviews the random photographs of vehicles that have caught his eye on the road. From these, he finds lines, shapes, and details that speak in visual terms to the themes embodied by the characters and story upon which the vehicle is to be based. Through that approach, he has done Hot Wheels based on *Ghostbusters*, *Back to the Future*, *The A-Team*, *The Flintstones*, *The Jetsons*, *The Simpsons*, *Scooby-Doo*, Snoopy, James Bond films, *Batman*, and others, in $\frac{1}{18}$, $\frac{1}{43}$, $\frac{1}{50}$, and $\frac{1}{64}$ scale.

His first Hot Wheels design, though, was a stock DeLorean. Mattel hadn't released one, and the production vehicle had been made so long before that there were no manufacturer files to work from. Cheung had to go off images, estimating ratios and proportions as he translated them on screen. He later bought a DeLorean, of which Mattel created a Hot Wheels version using special graphics.

The DeLorean enticed him for the same reasons as his later work. He wasn't obsessed with the specifications and performance figures. He just liked the shape.

Above: Mattel now owns the rights to the Batmobile, which it produces in multiple scales and beautiful finish and detail.

Chapter 3
PRODUCTION GOES GLOBAL

M atched against the competition, Mattel's car and track designs roared to the front of the pack. But while they surpassed the goals that had been set out for design, another challenge presented itself. The Mattel team needed to figure out a way to keep up with demand, and produce the cars on a global scale.

Ken Sanger's initial request of fifty million Hot Wheels for Kmart alone sounded like summiting Mount Everest. It would not be a request easily granted. Mattel had nothing close to that number available; neither did it have manufacturing capability on that scale. The company's projections had involved far fewer cars. Elliot had lobbied for ten million the first year, while Ruth and the rest of management had set the number at five million—or ten percent of the existing market.

If early fears were that no one would want the company's new toy, the panic as product launch drew near was that too many people were clamoring for it. Management upped its manufacturing target to a million Hot Wheels per week, or the equivalent of a thousand cars cast, assembled, painted, and packaged

for delivery a thousand times, every seven days. And that meant sellable cars that passed inspection without any discernible flaw.

Getting to that number was an Olympic-size hurdle, which began with the design itself. For the Handlers and the market, the toy needed to look like an automobile, certainly. But to be assembled in high volume, in molded form, it couldn't be an exact replica, as some traditional car components just wouldn't translate to a scaled-down version produced on a rapid-fire assembly line. Some alterations could be anticipated at the drawing stage. Other changes cropped up in the modeling process. Still further modifications, required to realize play value, did not present themselves until the product reached in-house testing or even consumers' hands.

The rollers presented a typical challenge. On a real car, it was the tire that touched the road, mounted to a wheel affixed to the hub. Early Hot Wheels had no separate tires; instead, the wheel was shaped and then painted to represent the wheel plus tire. The center of the outer face was formed like a spoked road wheel, after the

Opposite: Part of the Hot Wheels allure came from the Spectraflame paints. Equally important was the surface underneath—shiny zinc plating (over a casting of ZAMAC, an alloy of zinc, aluminum, magnesium, and copper). A 1971 Grass Hopper casting is shown here on its way to the electrostatic painting process.

custom rims on Harry Bradley's El Camino, while the outer portion served as the tire. Center spokes would be silver; the tire portion received a thin, red, circular stripe—a "redline." Set into the back of the piece was a Delrin low-friction bearing that rode on the wire axle.

To make a million cars a week, Mattel would have to create, paint, stripe, and fit bearings into four million wheels a week. Mattel's head of manufacturing, Frank Sesto, described the Delrin inserts as the size of a grain of rice—fussy to be worked with at all and particularly at that pace. Misplacing a single, small box could remove one hundred thousand bearings from production.

Die-casting was the logical technique for bodies, with a century of development behind it. The process was created in the mid-1800s, when it was used to form letters for printing machines. In ensuing decades, manufacturers made molds to cast parts for record players, cash registers, and other devices.

For metal objects, it was among the highest-volume production methods available, with many advantages at toy scale. While real car bodies use multiple panels that have to be welded, bolted, or hinged together, a die-cast Hot Wheels body is typically a single piece (for those without opening engine covers). It is swiftly formed by machines that force molten metal into precision molds, or dies, under high pressure. The pieces can be made in complex shapes, identically and swiftly, in large number. They are dimensionally stable, heat and impact resistant, and require little post-casting cleanup.

To produce millions, Mattel needed dies and casting machinery of huge capacity. Its initial plan was to manufacture all Hot Wheels at Hong Kong Industries (HKI), a seven-story factory complex that Mattel had purchased to make doll clothing for Barbie. After buying it, employees had discovered that the facility also held a small die-cast operation and tool room in one of the upper floors.

Sesto went overseas to determine whether those half-dozen machines could make the new small cars. They were old Battenfeld mechanically operated units. Sesto thought they might work, with some significant effort. He sent model maker Jack Hargreaves to HKI to test the concept.

The building manager in Hong Kong helped Hargreaves find local equipment to set up a model shop. Hargreaves decided to jump-start the die-making process by using ¹⁄₂₄-scale plastic-model bodies to create initial molds. Most of the road cars Mattel planned to emulate at miniature scale were available

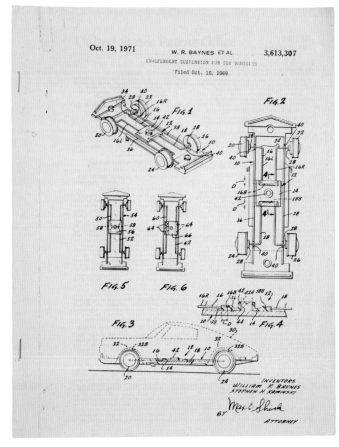

Top: This close-up of the 1967 Silhouette wheels shows the Delrin low-friction inner "wheel" that attached to the thin wire axle. **Bottom:** The early Hot Wheels axles were U-shaped, allowing sophisticated, independent suspension travel at each corner, as shown on this U.S. patent for Hot Wheels, 1971.

as glue-up hobby kits. Hargreaves bought a bunch and modified their plastic bodies to suit designers' lines and the die-cast process. He then used them to create epoxy molds of cars Bradley and his colleagues had designed, including a Camaro and Mustang.

From the oversize molds, the model maker cut dies to Hot Wheels scale using a pantograph. This device incorporates a jointed parallelogram to transpose lines from a traced object. One point on the pantograph follows the lines of the object. A drawing or cutting implement is placed elsewhere on the parallelogram. Depending on where it's placed, it can replicate the first object in bigger or smaller size. Hargreaves affixed a cutting tool and used the pantograph to cut Hot Wheels–sized dies from the $\frac{1}{24}$-scale molds he had made from the plastic models.

He hired six local craftsmen to help him, which introduced a new challenge in addressing the language barrier. Mattel's

onsite interpreters knew both spoken languages but not engineering terminology. Translating among the different vocabularies produced numerous complications and delays. At the same time, Mattel headquarters was making changes to the design conception that required additional modifications in Hong Kong.

Hargreaves had started out with fixed, rigid axles, like other die-cast miniature makers were using at the time. He sized his wheel openings accordingly. After he and his team had produced two or three sample cars they felt were looking pretty good, the California engineers came up with the thin-wire axles, allowing a small-car version of suspension travel. This forced Hargreaves' team to remake their molds to allow wheel movement without interference from tiny fenders.

The hazards were not merely economic. The Battenfeld machines used a mechanical clamping action to hold the dies together when the hot metal was forced

---

Above: The Handlers and Matt Matson started Mattel as Mattel Creations in Los Angeles, CA, in 1945. After Matson sold his share, the company became Mattel, Inc., in 1948. It maintained its Hawthorne headquarters shown here for about thirty years. In 1989 the press learned that Mattel was negotiating for property in nearby El Segundo, where it moved from this long-serving location.

Utility operator Eulah Smith in Hot Wheels is the center of interest for a group of French businessmen during a recent tour of Plant 1.

MILLION CAR WEEK
MARCH 24-28, 1969
1,000,001TH CAR PRODUCED ON
3-28-69
HOT WHEELS-HAWTHORNE, CALIF.

in—versus hydraulic pressure in newer equipment. If not clamped tightly, molten alloy could be displaced to surfaces where it did not belong. Such residue, when not cleaned away, would cause a gap through which liquid metal could escape in a subsequent casting. The heat from the spill was intense enough to burn a hole through a worker's leather shoes.

By the time Hargreaves and his craftsmen had made a couple thousand cars, management concluded that the old machines at HKI could not produce cars of the quality and quantity Mattel needed. His modeling efforts were shipped back to the United States and used by other shops to make dies for cars they would manufacture on contract.

A & A Die Casting Company and H & H Injection Molding Company were two stateside manufacturers lined up for production. A & A was to make Hot Wheels bodies, and H & H would create the plastic interiors. Initial discussions involved hiring the firms. When it became clear that Mattel's production demands would use the full capacity of both entities, however, it bought H & H, then A & A.

Still hoping to make use of its Hong Kong facility for manufacturing, Mattel devised a plan. It would develop the tooling necessary for each model at its Hawthorne, California, plant, operate it for a few months to get it functioning smoothly, and then transport it to HKI for long-term production. The California plant would then tool up for another model and repeat the process. Demand for Hot Wheels outpaced the strategy, however. Rather than disassembling equipment and shipping it

across the Pacific Ocean, Mattel was forced to build duplicate machinery at the overseas plant and keep the Hawthorne operation humming at full tilt.

Along with the four wheels, die-cast body, and injection-molded plastic interior, the typical vehicle has a chassis, axle system, and a windshield/windows piece. It all has to be assembled, inspected, packaged, and shipped out, again and again, at a relentless pace—requiring a vast workforce. New hires streamed into Mattel by the dozens, daily. They were told to expect atypical days off to accommodate the nearly 'round-the-clock, seven-days-a-week operation.

By late summer 1968, the Hawthorne plant, near Los Angeles, had almost three thousand workers employed in fifty assembly lines completing Hot Wheels. Nearly five hundred additional employees performed quality inspections. As of November, the warehouse had some 5,600 assemblers preparing Hot Wheels for shipping over three shifts a day. Finally, in December, the month of the massive sales rush, Mattel hit its target of a million cars a week. Still, demand ran so high that consumers called the company into the night and lined up at the factory gate, seeking to buy directly to fulfill their children's wish lists. There simply were not enough Hot Wheels on site, or in existence, to satisfy the market.

Left: Utility operator Eulah Smith exemplified Mattel's attention to detail during a tour of Hawthorne's Plant I by French business visitors, circa 1969. **Right:** The goal of a million cars a week became a necessity as demand soared following the initial release.

Top left: Hot Wheels vehicle bodies stacked fresh from the die-cast tooling, circa 1970s. **Top right:** Mattel's production line itself evoked the car-on-a-track excitement that set Hot Wheels apart. **Bottom:** Not every car could make it as a Hot Wheels. Quality Control employed professional fault-finders to keep vehicles with blemishes, breakage, missing details, or missing parts from releasing to stores.

A MILLION

The toy-manufacturing process many children are first exposed to bears no resemblance to the actual operation. It involves a silver-haired fellow, named Claus, operating out of a workshop with a team of elves. They make all the toys delivered globally by Claus himself through an antiquated flying-sleigh/rooftop/chimney approach on Christmas Eve. Lots of kids have been told that their Hot Wheels came to them in this way.

Current data from Mattel differs, at least as told to grown-ups. This information suggests that none of the company's die-cast vehicles are presently made in the North Pole or anywhere within the Arctic Circle. Rather, the main plant is five thousand miles south, in Penang, Malaysia. HS Lee, a man with many years of experience at Mattel, runs the facility. He has helped increase output from about one hundred thousand cars per day to a million a day.

The once-a-year delivery in the Claus system would not work for Lee. His operation is outfitted for manufacturing, with limited space for storage. There is nowhere near enough room to house the annual output of more than three hundred million cars. Finished product is shipped out continuously on a daily basis. The toys leave Malaysia by sea in shipping containers that hold about three hundred thousand Hot Wheels apiece. From there, a multiplatform system carries them to regional distribution centers for delivery to retailers around the world.

The factory uses a discrete process, in which a variety of machines perform different operations to make the six components that comprise a typical car: the body, chassis, interior, window piece, and a pair of "dumbbells"—axles with wheels. The bodies are usually die cast—though chassis can be either plastic or die cast—and the interiors, window, and wheels are plastic (except when tires are

Above: While early production came from Hong Kong and Hawthorne, CA, the primary Hot Wheels plant today is in Penang, Malaysia. It raised the million-a-week production mark of old to a million a day!

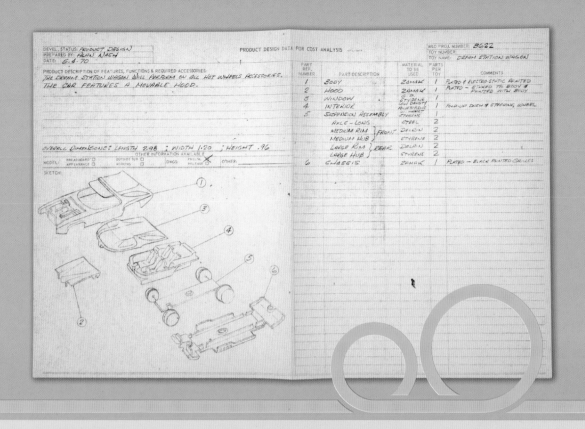

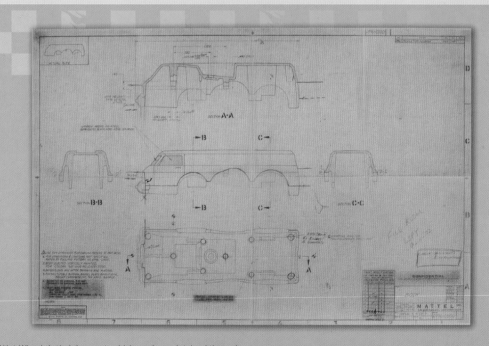

HOT WHEELS A DAY

Top: One key trait of Hot Wheels is their low cost, which can be maintained through analysis of production requirements. This sheet breaks out components for a design proposed in 1970. **Bottom:** Blueprint for a Reger, a Hot Wheels offshoot, 1972. Original Hot Wheels documents used in design and production are prized by collectors.

synthetic-rubber Real Riders). Main processes include die casting, plating, injection molding, vacuum metalizing, painting, pad printing, assembly, and packing.

Four thousand plant workers operate about one thousand machines to perform these various manufacturing functions. They work in three rotating shifts, with more than one thousand employees on-site at one time.

Model changes are common. In a given week, the facility averages about two hundred different vehicles, including variations. It makes eight hundred to nine hundred different models over the course of a year. This variety allows choices for customers, including autos specific to particular markets. Each model change works its way through the multistage manufacturing process. Switching tooling for a new body takes only about fifteen to thirty minutes. A minimum batch size will then be run, which takes about four hours for each process. A completed minimum batch of new models can be manufactured in sisteen to twenty-four hours. On average, the facility produces twelve cars a second.

Supplying toys to kids around the world is a wonderful opportunity that Mattel values. To do so smoothly involves navigating many challenges—different languages, cultures, economies, and infrastructures. Decisions made at Mattel headquarters affect the efforts of people working not only on different continents but different days. If Scott Goodman calls Lee at 5:00 p.m. Monday from California, Lee's half of the conversation is occurring at 8:00 a.m. Tuesday in Penang.

Like Lee, Goodman has a long and cherished tenure at Mattel—more than thirty years. A point of pride is the regular task force Mattel's leadership has put together with overseas collaborators since the late 1980s. The purpose is to meet face-to-face, as colleagues and friends, and not solely over phone calls and video conferences. These meetings have strengthened relationships. They have also made decision making more organic, flowing from a deeper knowledge and appreciation of the other players involved, plus their skills and insights and the job complications they confront. Thus, if the company wanted to change the color of a car from blue to green or apply more chrome through a vacuum-metallizing process, the insights gained through the task forces allow a better understanding of the implications of those changes, reducing inconvenience and delays.

Above: Mattel's Bangkok facility was producing Matchbox cars when Mattel acquired that company in 1998.

In a highly competitive market like toys, efficiency is key. Safe, streamlined processes keep costs low and quality high. Still, consistency is a balancing act in which parts wear and technologies improve. Both within Mattel and far beyond, research and development continues on manufacturing techniques, process automation, equipment, and materials. Lee's plant sets benchmarks for its machines to facilitate planning and budgeting for improvements.

Goodman enjoys keeping Hot Wheels the number one die-cast car in the world, driving from the front like the rider at the head of the Tour de France peloton. He considers it sport, and as with any serious sport, it can be stressful. He's wary of a competitor stepping up with a faster car and is ever vigilant for ways to head that off. Competition suits his nature, as does Mattel—winning a toy-design contest sponsored by the company at his university helped him land his first work there as a summer intern.

Now he and Lee are colleagues, collaborating to make the manufacture of Hot Wheels the best it can be. Their decades with the company form a firm foundation of knowledge and experience, plus familiarity with methods and scenarios that have affected productivity. They also value fresh perspectives. New employees bring new ideas—and reexamination of old ones, which can become so routine their suitability to improvement fades from view. A recent plant opening in Indonesia provided the opportunity to share best practices as well as take a clean-slate look at setting up a modern facility.

Lee, Goodman, and others immersed in the manufacturing process have shared goals. They seek the highest-quality Hot Wheels product at a price that keeps it accessible to children everywhere. As Lee puts it, he wants the cars to be the coolest-looking out there, the fastest if they compete, and the most durable through the drops and crashes and stunts that are inevitable with active play.

That sentiment is shared by all Mattel employees. They're not elves in Santa's fabled shop. They're thousands of workers devoted to making Hot Wheels—a million a day.

Above: Mattel's Bangkok facility is capable of turning out over 100 million Hot Wheels cars per year.

VELOCITY ON DISPLAY

Before Hot Wheels, the king in die-cast miniatures was Matchbox. True to the name, the cars were about the size of a box of wooden matches. Likewise, they were sold in a small box, with an image of the contents printed on it. As it did with its new product's performance, Mattel wanted more from the packaging.

Great products are said to sell themselves. To enhance his speedsters' sales pitch, Elliot thought youngsters should see the brightly painted hot rods Mattel had created for them. Rather than cardboard boxes, he wanted a package type that had appeared in cosmetics but was not yet common with toys. A blister pack could hold a Hot Wheels vehicle in transparent plastic, enticing customers with a clear look at the very thing they would be vrooming over track and table when they got it home.

His direction went still further. Not only should shoppers see Mattel's small car, they should see it anywhere merchants had space for it. For stores with pegs, the carton should hang, ripe fruit for the picking. If the seller had shelves, the same package should stand up straight in neat rows for ogling and comparison. Finally, the graphics on the printed cardboard backing had to capture Hot Wheels excitement. Production, of course, would have to keep pace with the cars themselves.

Common with an Elliot idea, there was no predecessor to the package he wanted. Other blisters were symmetrical, and that's what existing vacuum-form tooling was designed to create. To make a cardboard-backed blister stand vertically, however, a symmetrical container with 90-degree corners wouldn't work if it were attached all the way around by a glued-down flange. That configuration would lean forward until the lower front of the blister was the same level as the bottom of the cardboard to which the blister was glued.

The solution, viewing the standing package from the front, was to shift the outer face of the blister and angle its bottom side downward. This allowed the lower leading edge of the blister to touch the shelf along with the bottom of the backing board in a manner that supported the backing vertically. Angling the bottom downward had the additional benefit of tilting the car forward so that kids could view both the profile and top sides easily.

A resulting complication was that the blister was now "sided," with a defined top and bottom. To come off the forming surface, it would need to be pulled at an angle or the base surface would have to be tilted. To meet its numbers, Mattel needed each machine to make about twenty blisters at a shot. It was just another necessity soon to mother an invention.

Left: Matchbox's approach to packaging had a classy simplicity, and provided an enduring way to protect the cars, but the design looked antique. **Right:** Mattel's flashy packaging included a clear blister to show off the car. While both packages were from the 1960s, Mattel's appeared futuristic at the time.

The cars' gem of a backing card was similarly formed from creativity under pressure. Graphic designer Rick Irons was asked to handle the design. At the time, merchandise sold in blister packs used rectangular backing cards. Irons thought a different shape would stand out. He tried a horizontal S-curve across the top. Mattel had settled on a hot-rod theme for its new small cars. Hand-painted flames was a racy stylistic touch Irons had seen on some modified rides. This flowing fire was a welcome addition to the curved cardboard backing.

Most of the product elements were now in place, except for the final name. Mattel was still referring to the cars as California Customs. At seventeen letters, that title was too long for Irons to shape into letters readable across a toy store. The problem solved itself when management chose "Hot Wheels" instead. Those nine letters would be legible, and the heat theme suited his flame concept. Adding red and orange hues would catch toy-browsing eyes while reinforcing the bright colors of the cars behind the bubbles.

For imagery to accompany the logo, Irons hired an outside illustrator. Otto Kuhni made artistic automobile sketches with a Hot Wheels feel, which Irons inserted below the flaming letters.

Each blister pack also held a metal badge of the car purchased, which Mattel thought kids would clip to their shirts or belts to show off their favorite models.

With design dialed and production at full rip, Mattel hit the die-cast car market with foot flat on the go pedal. The company's desire to give Hot Wheels the most play value of any toy car on the market was a commitment from which it would never let up. Over the ensuing years, that drive would make Hot Wheels the best-selling toy in the world, with enough variety, accessories, and excitement to keep small-car fans playing, marveling, and collecting for a lifetime.

Ralph Parris, an industrial engineer, and Bill Robb, a tooling engineer, conceived a saw-toothed forming surface (or platen) with the rows flipped. This angled the downward-sloping blister bottoms toward one another so that the blister walls were formed parallel. The batch could then be pulled off a machine at once. Parris showed the single-blister prototype to a vacuum-forming expert visiting the factory from DuPont, then said he needed to make many like that at one time. The visitor interjected that it wasn't possible, so Parris led him to the production facility. There, fitted with Parris and Robb's platens, machines were churning out about one hundred thousand blister packs per shift. DuPont's man was impressed.

Left: The original stand Hot Wheels were sold from, 1968. Large eye-catching displays made customers aware of new cars. A catalog helped fans create their "wishlist." **Right:** The original 1970s Hot Wheels logo evoked hot rods and hand-painted flames.

California Custom Miniatures
Python. "First Sixteen," 1968

Flying Colors
Mercedes-Benz C-111, 1974

Flying Colors
'57 Chevy, 1977

Oldies But Goodies
Auburn 852, 1979

HiRakers
40's Woodie, 1980

1981 Hot Wheels
Old Number 5, 1981

Real Riders
Classic Cobra, 1983

The earliest version of the Hot Wheels logo featured the tagline, "Fastest metal cars in the world!" Soon, it changed to "Hottest metal cars in the world!" And before too long, the tagline was dropped altogether. Later flames were added. The basic packaging and background would also see their own evolution with each new year and each new series. Here is a small sample from various Hot Wheels over the years that shows the subtle variations and the thoughtfulness that go into each car's packaging.

Trailbusters
Path Beater, 1986

Speed Fleet
Porsche 959, 1988

Classics
'32 Ford Delivery, 1989

Main Line
Purple Passion, 1990

First Editions
Scorchin Scooter, 1997

Main Line
Hot Seat, 1999

Digital Circuit
Winning Formula, 2016

Muscle Mania
Muscle Speeder, 2016

Nightburnerz
'17 Nisson GT-R35, 2017

Race Team
Twinduction, 2014

#6978 MERCEDES C-111
#7618 WINNIPEG™
#7622 GRASS HOPPER®
#8260 STEAM ROLLER®

#6980 ICE 'T'®
#7619 HEAVY® CHEVY
#7630 TOP ELIMINATOR®
#8261 SIR RODNEY ROADSTER™

#7616 RASH I™
#7620 VOLKSWAGEN
#8258 BAJA BRUISER™
#8262 BREAKAWAY BUCKET™

TAMPO PRINTING

Quality, authenticity, variety . . . Hot Wheels' success turned on these traits. Just as full-size street cars, race cars, and work trucks feature stripes, numbers, logos, and business names, so too would Mattel's growing line of miniatures. Any such decoration would have to look and function at the same uncompromising standards as every other aspect of the design—and be capable of consistent, cost-effective replication in dizzying numbers.

On real vehicles and plastic kits, such flourishes could be hand-painted or added with decals or stickers. None of these options was ideal at Hot Wheels scale. The price point was too low and the volume too high for hand-painting to work on mass-produced models—even though the technique was sometimes employed to design prototypes.

Decals or stickers would have needed printing, cutting, and application—and then to survive the rigors of packaging and shipping—to arrive in good condition.

From there, challenges would have increased, as the words and logo decals were subjected to rough play and harsh environments. These forces would have caused decals to crack and flake off and stickers to shift, fade, and feather, and attract dirt along their edges. Decay would have turned cool enhancements into bummer blemishes.

Mattel could have offered replacement stickers and decals, but that approach still required kids—or patient parents—to set aside play for the role of miniature auto-body technician. And the result might look no better.

The answer to great graphics was an old technique to which Hot Wheels had a historic connection. Their bodies were die-cast, a technology used for printing-press letters in the mid-1800s. Before that, the china industry had developed an ink-transfer method to put intricate designs on plates. Their crafters engraved patterns in copper, then filled the impressions with ink. Using a soft pad, a worker

Above: A sample of the many shapes, images, lines, numbers, and colors tampo made possible.

would then transfer the ink by pressing the pad first on the copper engraving and then onto the china plate.

In the 1950s, Swiss watchmakers adopted a manual printing technique. They would engrave and ink the hours and minutes pattern for a timepiece and use a pad to press it on to a watch face. In the following decade, a man named Wilfried Philipp created the pad-printing machine in Germany. That development has led to the widespread use of pad printing in many industries around the world, on computer keyboards and cables, appliances, sports equipment, and many other products, including toys.

The crucial feature for these industries, including Mattel, is the pad. Whereas direct printing presses the item onto the inked pattern itself, like letters against paper, pad printing uses a flexible tool for the transfer. The pad picks up the ink and applies it, distorting as necessary to make full contact with the receiving object. Pad printing can make clear numbers, letters, and lines on wavy, curved, or round surfaces.

Pad, or tampo, printing was perfect for Hot Wheels. The flexible pad could apply symbols, logos, and monikers to an expansive variety of shapes, including miniature doors, hoods, fenders, trunks, beds, and tankers, whether it be a race-car number or longtime designer Larry Wood's actual home phone number, a design joke that inadvertently wasn't revised before the toy hit the shelves. And it could produce them in durable form at high volume. Mattel launched the first cars created through this printing process in 1974.

The machines do have to be set up properly and monitored to keep pace. Silicone pads, which are durable and flexible and release ink well, have long since replaced their gelatin predecessors. The inks need proper viscosity for good coverage, and the size, shape, application mechanics, and pad hardness must be well-suited to the object to be printed. Thin concentration must be maintained. And static electricity, which can build to thousands of volts and attract dust and other impurities, must be dissipated.

Mattel's engineers carefully adjust the machines for each vehicle and pattern design. Done as such, the payoff is high. Tampo printing has adorned hundreds of millions of die-cast miniatures—at least—and continues to serve the Hot Wheels fleet.

CLEAR ACROSS THE CURVES

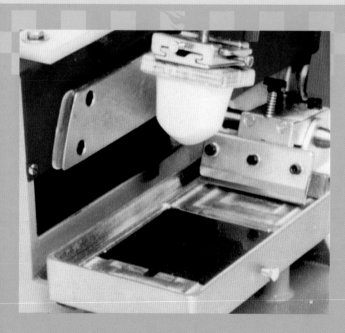

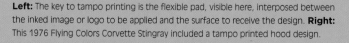

Left: The key to tampo printing is the flexible pad, visible here, interposed between the inked image or logo to be applied and the surface to receive the design. **Right:** This 1976 Flying Colors Corvette Stingray included a tampo printed hood design.

Peterbilt Hauler, 1981

GMC Hauler, 1981

Peterbilt Tanker, 1981

Kentworth Van, 1981

Tampo printing allowed Hot Wheels trucks to be customized. Starting in the early 1980s, Hot Wheels Steering Rigs featured a clear knob at the back of the trailer or tanker that would turn the rig when rotated. Steering worked via a vertical pin moving in a semicircular slot around the trailer's or tanker's hitch. The Steering Rigs also featured a piece of rubber on a set of the wheels to give the wheels grip. Without it, turning the knob would have no effect.

COLOR HIGHLIGHTS

The ability to go unseen is critical to survival in the animal kingdom. In the toy world, however, it's just the opposite. Failure to capture the public's eye means extinction. When Hot Wheels entered the market in 1968, there were not only thousands of various playthings competing for attention, there were countless toy cars and trucks of nearly every size, color, and shape that makers could imagine—*nearly*.

Bright candy colors had found their ways onto real cars in the custom scene more than a decade before, and yet at handheld scale, the colorful fleets on department store shelves appeared plain—not necessarily of poor quality, or inaccurate compared to production models, just . . . ordinary. To Mattel, that subdued exterior, while only a millimeter thick, left room for innovation.

Spectraflame paint was a breakthrough for the new toy market entrant, taking die-cast car finish in a

fresh direction that demanded attention. Hot Wheels' Spectraflame colors used both the casting itself along with the paint to achieve a radiance that seemed to pull in light, ramp up its wattage, and then beam it back even bolder than any other toy of the time.

In a typical paint job, the metal is first sprayed with primer, which is a dull, tacky coating to which the brighter topcoat will adhere. The opaque primer blankets the shiny metal and prevents light from reaching it. The car's shine with that approach comes from the clear-coating that is applied on top of the paint. Mattel's Spectraflame paints, originally used from 1968 to 1972, kept the car's metal surface in visual play.

Spectraflame Hot Wheels did not receive primer. Instead, the metal surface was polished and hit directly with a translucent color coat. Because the paint was translucent, rather than opaque, light passed through the

Above: The magic of Spectraflame, shown here on the Custom Camaro.

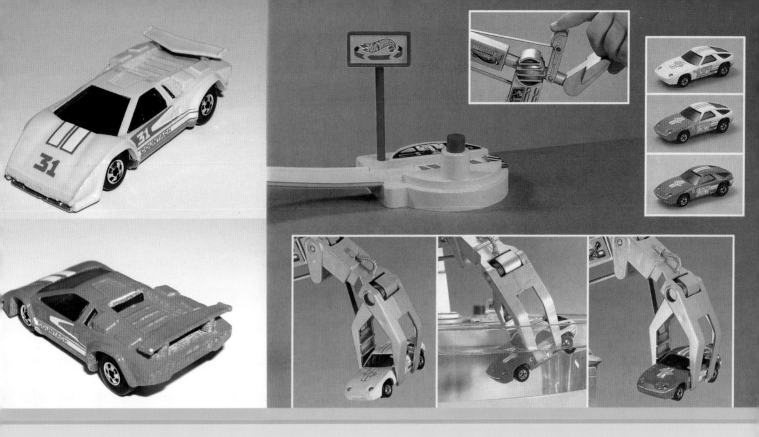

SPECTRAFLAME TO COLOR SHIFTERS

finish, struck the polished metal surface, and passed back through the paint to convey a gleaming eye-catching shine.

The brilliant colors were a smash hit for Mattel, setting its new die-casts apart from all competitors. Each model was available in a range of colors. An early Spectraflame Color Guide, for example, identified purple, lavender, red, orange, gold, brown, olive, lime, green, aqua, light blue, and blue as available colors. Within each of those colors, differences in the paint mixture, supplier, application, and the brightness of the Hot Wheels' underlying metal finish created variation in the final appearance. Over time, exposure to sunlight and other environmental influences further altered the color range.

These factors, along with terms used by the Hot Wheels community, expanded the range of names for Spectraflame colors to include descriptions like watermelon, rose, magenta, salmon, berry, antifreeze,

ice blue, Windex blue, apple green, light green, copper, creamy pink, and hot pink. Due to the range in appearance, it's not uncommon for fans to disagree over what shade actually adorns a particular car. In the end, such variety increases the opportunity to find and enjoy unique shades.

Market and regulatory factors ended the original Spectraflame era in 1972, yet the appeal of the finish has brought revivals of the look from both Mattel and the fan base. Mattel has offered modern Spectraflame colors in the Hot Wheels Classics line, launched in 2005; Super Treasure Hunt models, beginning in 2007; Red Line Club vehicles, beginning in 2006; and through HotWheelsCollectors.com in an online exclusive series, beginning in 2002.

Hands-on die-cast lovers have also embraced the Spectraflame look, performing restorations and customizations with their own admiring community of followers on websites like Instagram. These crafters

Above: Color Changers changed the game. This ad shows how to use hot and cold water to change the color of the car's body.

strip tired, boring, or damaged finishes, polish the underlying casting, and hand-spray their Hot Wheels to achieve a Spectraflame look. Several paint manufacturers offer translucent colors, and Mattel has partnered with PPG to produce a Spectraflame line in aqua, medium sapphire, lime gold, bright emerald, antifreeze green, orange, bright red, Hot Wheels blue, hot pink, light red watermelon, and purple. As with Mattel's 21st Century Spectraflame Hot Wheels, the approach to these hand-sprayed finishes differs from what the early cars used, but it can provide outstanding shine when applied with skill.

Spectraflame was a fresh look when it flashed into stores, but Mattel's innovators don't coast on success.

Color Racers (1988), Color FX (1993), and Color Shifters (2008) brought new levels of play to Hot Wheels, with paints that fans could alter at once by heating or cooling the finish with hot or cold water. The temperature change shifted the paint molecules, causing them to reflect a different portion of the light spectrum. Evolutions of this technology led to greater color variety and shine, hidden details that emerged with a temperature change, and even a shift to glow-in-the-dark shades.

New innovation and creativity within Mattel's walls and among its worldwide fan base are sure to keep the fresh looks coming, in ways that are no more foreseeable now than when Spectraflame paints appeared in toy stores half a century ago.

Above: The Hot Wheels Color Shifters Flame Play Set, released in 2014, is full of color-changing transformation, excitement, and mayhem. **Opposite:** Hot Wheels Color Changers cover a wide range of color and design.

Timeline of Cars

1968
The Custom Camaro is the first of the "Sweet Sixteen" to be produced by Hot Wheels.

1969
The rare pink rear-loading Volkswagen Beach Bomb prototype.

1981
The Hot Ones, with thinner wheels for faster speed, are introduced.

1983
The Real Riders, with real rubber tires, are introduced.

1960s **1970s** **1990s**

1970
The Sizzlers spin-off line is introduced, along with the popular Snake and Mongoose funny cars.

1980s

1988
The release of Color Changers changed everything by altering the paint color with temperature, such as the Ferrari 308 that changed from pink to white.

1991
The Billionth Car Collection is released, trophy-style, with the 1970's casting of the Corvette Stingray.

1974
The Flying Colors car series is introduced.

1984
The Baja Bug is released into the Hot Wheels lineup.

1995
The Hot Wheels line is split up into series, including select vehicles packaged as Treasure Hunt cars.

2006
The Bone Shaker, based on Larry Wood's design, is released.

1997
Hot Wheels makes a deal with NASCAR and begins making scale models of NASCAR stock cars.

2008
The $140,000 Diamond Car kicks off Hot Wheels fortieth anniversary at Toy Fair.

2011
The *Back to the Future* Time Machine, modeled after the film's popular DeLorean DMC-12, is released.

2000s

2002
Hot Wheels debuts Monster Jam Trucks at World Finals 3 as well as introduces the exclusive online Red Line club for collectors.

2009
The Dragstrip Demons series is released. The series continued for two years.

2010s

2018
To celebrate the 50th anniversary of Hot Wheels, Chevrolet created a 2018 Custom Camaro and Mattel released the $1/64$-scale version.

2005
Hot Wheels Classics Series 1 is introduced, including this '40s Woodie.

Chapter 4

BEYOND THE CARS

When you craft toys, not every formidable hurdle in your path has the austere gravity of the adult world. Yes, there are stresses, competitors, and uncertainties to wrestle, but every new product also requires Mattel's team to answer a gleeful, even childish, question: *Is it epic?*

That's the beauty of a job making toys. Mattel's designers and engineers are research scientists in the abstract field of play.

It's fascinating yet also demanding work, a world not bound by conventional rules. Children at play are oblivious to logic or laws that stop "real" objects from moving as toys do in their imaginary realm. Telling kids that Hot Wheels without engines or wings can't fly or drive up a wall or leap the gap between the coffee table and the hearth makes no sense when they've been doing those things all morning. Toys are produced within constraints of science and economics but enjoyed by a population whose fanciful landscapes recognize no such limits.

Fortunately at Mattel, it's a stimulating, fulfilling quest, backed by an employer that encourages its employees

to maximize resourcefulness and imagination in pursuit of creating an immersive experience that will delight and inspire its fans. That freedom has produced a broad array of innovations that have expanded the Hot Wheels universe in size, capability, and reach.

Opposite: This 1970s Hot Wheels Action Accessories ad focused on the tracks and cases to augment the cars. The toy market evolves rapidly, with manufacturers and the press ever vigilant for the next new thing. **Right:** This ad for the Hot Wheels Flying Colors Double Dare track won customers over.

GRAVITY DEFYING

Elliot and his brain squad created Hot Wheels, but gravity was their driving force. Gravity power had major perks. It was free, always on, and never ran out. Unleash a Hot Wheels car atop an inclined track and it was going to dash away, every time—fast. That was the elemental leap Elliot had hunted, the breakaway trait his brilliant tinkerers served up.

Unfortunately, friction was just as powerful. Everywhere gravity heaped on speed like a sprinting bobsled team shoving on a sled, friction waited at the bottom of the hill to put its meddlesome foot on the brakes. When the incline disappeared, the pace did too. The cars slowed until rolling resistance dragged them to a halt.

This never stopped another run or a third or a fiftieth. Yet it did engage imaginations in considering ways to keep the wheels whipping. To a group of engineers and scientists, toy propulsion was adult-sized play. Applying rubber bands, electric motors, foam wheels, magnets, rotors, and remote controls, the big kids at Mattel found a host of ways for Hot Wheels to stay speedy.

Elastic bands were a speed enhancer available to employees without getting up from the desk, so it's no surprise that this arm's-reach resource found its way onto the Hot Wheels scene. The Rod Runner Hand Shift Power-Booster resembles an automotive floor shifter with orange track run through the bottom. Pushing the lever forward stretches a rubber band while pulling back a thrust arm that locks into place above car height. Roll a Hot Wheels into the booster and it releases the arm, which the rubber band draws down swiftly into the back of the car, launching it down the straightaway. Mattel has offered other rubber-powered boosters that start cars from rest, flinging them at the push of a button or lever.

Hot Wheels Revvers (launched in the 1970s) and the later Speed Winders provide in-board elastic-cord go. The band runs lengthwise down the center of the car. Turning a dial or crank twists the band(s), storing potential energy. Release the car, and like a rubber band–powered balsa plane, the uncoiling band drives the wheels and the car across the floor. As with inclination, when the twist ends, so does the boost.

Rev-Ups feature another time-tested drivetrain, the friction push motor, combined with magnetic force. The combination permits the vehicles to climb vertical walls and traverse inverted surfaces. The friction motors drive the wheels with a lower-speed and torquier action, more like heavy equipment than race technology.

Above: Gravity's pull was the original power source for Hot Wheels. Making them run on level ground was the next step. Options were the same as for a full-size vehicle—either shove it externally or use an internal drive mechanism with the Hand Shift Power-Booster (right) or the Revvers (left).

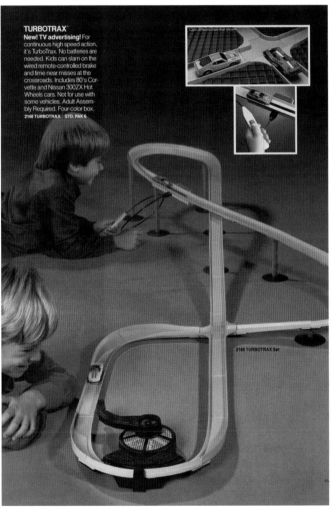

Cars different from that shown.

2148 TURBOTRAX Set

Batteries, the old toy mainstay, provide juice for much longer duration. The Hot Wheels team wasted no time applying power cells to its new fleet. The Super-Charger Race Set, first released in 1969, offers external boost via compressible foam-rimmed wheels spun toward one another by an electric motor. The foam wheels grab entering Hot Wheels of appropriate width and spit them out the other side, down a section of track passing through the Super-Charger.

A pair of Super-Chargers on opposite sides of an oval circuit can keep cars running laps for as long as they stay on the track, a condition influenced by the units' adjustable speed control.

On-board rechargeable batteries were not long behind. Sizzlers mimic real cars, driven by electric motors without wires or a slot car's pin, over straights, curves, loops, and jumps. Because the power source moves with the cars, Sizzlers maintain near constant speed, circling their plastic circuits much like full-size race cars do at race courses around the world. The miniature cars' onboard power cells can be recharged from larger batteries within a portable Goose Pump, a gas pump–shaped Juice Machine, or a service-stationlike Power Pit, which also exists in AC-plug form. Sizzlers can run at serious scaled speeds—hundreds of miles per hour—for minutes at a time.

Naturally, Mattel also got in on wireless, remote-control vehicles and the nuances afforded by the microchip age. The Ai Intelligent Race System uses battery-powered cars and controllers, plus a thin film track fitted with sensors. While the cars receive speed and directional input from the players' handsets, the vehicles also monitor the track itself and can provide contestants with different levels of assistance to stay on the circuit. The easiest settings are similar to full-size, self-driving cars, while at the most challenging level, only modest corrections kick in. There are no slots and no magnetic attraction, so players can maneuver anywhere on the track, or off it, depending on the level of assist selected. The Ai system may be raced with up to four live players and many computer-controlled competitors guided by the artificial intelligence program.

The most complete abandonment of gravity's influence comes from the Sky Shock remote-control car/plane hybrid. Like the ultimate James Bond vehicle, the Sky Shock can race over the ground as an automobile, lift off and fly like an aircraft, and then land and continue moving in wheeled, overland mode—in the hands of a skillful operator.

Top: The Hot Wheels A.i. uses computer-enhanced Artificial Intelligence to help guide your car around the track. **Bottom:** The TurboTrax system includes an arm that gives a push from behind as the cars round a corner. A hand-activated brake allows racers to slow the cars (or not) to alter the time they cross paths at an intersection on the course.

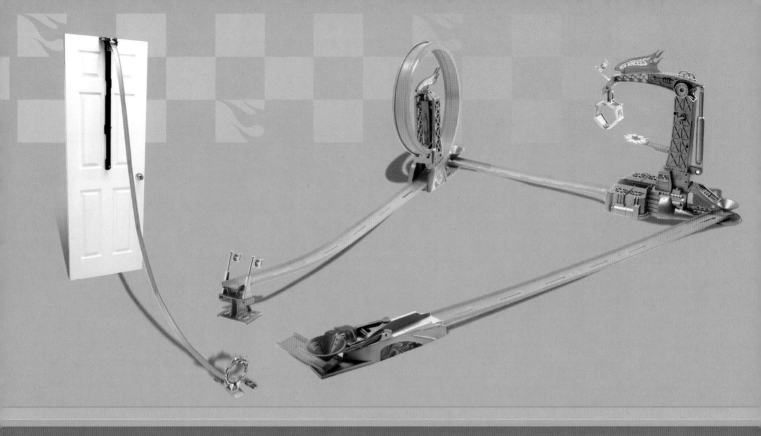

TRACKS & PLAY SETS

Hot Wheels are a different world. They had to be, because the trait they brought to market—namely speed—needed a venue. What the slower competitors on the market had to offer was the same, regardless of the surface they bumbled over, be it asphalt or concrete, a sandbox or a rug.

Introducing a blazing toy car to driveways and dirt patches would have been like delivering world-class surfboards to the middle of the Sahara. Yes, Hot Wheels looked different, with their hot-rod mods and brilliant paint. But their enhanced play value lay in performance. With scaled speeds exceeding two hundred miles per hour, Hot Wheels were faster than their full-size counterparts oozing bravado and horsepower.

Race cars need racetracks. Mattel knew this early in the game. As soon as Elliot's velocity crew realized how quick their creations would be, they designed

surfaces, shapes, stunts, and accessories to tap the cars' full potential. For five decades, the mission to build a Lilliputian world of fast-flying fun has evolved alongside design of the cars themselves. It's a ceaseless challenge of innovation and one-upmanship that the folks in Tracks and Play Sets wouldn't trade. They've brought diverse skills to Mattel to push themselves and their colleagues.

From a young age, Brendon Vetuskey puzzled over how things worked. Dismantle-and-discover was familiar behavior. He took apart toys, bikes, and snowmobiles to see what was going on in there. His grandfather had been an inventor for Kodak, and another relative had created the bicycle coaster brake.

Vetuskey began college with an interest in automotive design, but his passion was hot rods and muscle cars. Those vehicles didn't seem to merge with new market

Above: The Hot Wheels V-Drop Super Velocity Track Set (left) uses the back of a door and gravity to reach extreme speeds. The Trick Tracks Triple Stunt Starter set (right) features three interchangeable stunts that could be connected in different combinations.

trends, so he switched to product design. His mechanical inclination brought important perspective to the program's courses in product manufacturing, aesthetics, and ergonomics. It was perfect training to become part of the Tracks and Play Sets team.

To be viable for stores across the country and around the world, the designs that emerge from Tracks and Play Sets must account for all of these variables. Fifty years of innovation offers a lot to draw upon, yet it's demanding to find a fresh take. Vetuskey came in on the second season of Trick Tracks, little stunt parks that kids could assemble and vary. He added dinosaurs to one set and robots to another, integrating the additions to the cars' tests and trajectories. In one instance, the cars descend down the long neck, back, and tail of an Apatosaurus; in another, the flipperlike foot of a Mosasaurus is the ram that accelerates the vehicle.

Vetuskey also developed the 4-Lane Elimination Race and the Super 6-Lane Raceway. In the former, the lead car in each pair of adjacent lanes trips a switch that flips the

trailing car off the course. The four lanes then merge to two with the lead car ejecting the runner-up in the same way before funneling alone into a finish lane. The six-lane raceway features an overhead finish arch that illuminates the winning car's lane number and also announces it with an audio track that mimics stadium sound. The six lanes fold up for compact storage and are simple enough for a young child to operate. Mattel maintains variety by moving sets in and out of the marketplace. It's a point of pride for Vetuskey to find the six-lane raceway selling used online for far more than it cost new.

Paul Schmid took a different path to the team. His parents thought an engineering degree would set off his smile nicely when he went to look for a job. The best he could find of interest in that field was an ocean engineering program at Florida Institute of Technology. An intriguing opportunity arose to work on James Cameron's sci-fi sea film, *The Abyss*, building models for the characters' dive suits. Schmid followed that with models for *Total Recall*. Other film and TV projects came next, plus a stint at Disney

OFF THE WALL, AND NOT

Above: The Super 6-Lane Raceway included eight feet of classic track, along with lights and sounds at the finish line.

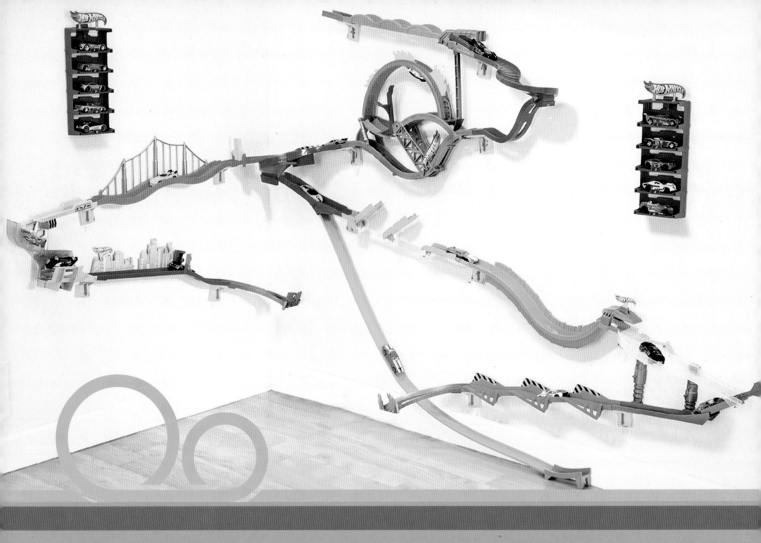

doing production design for its theme parks in California and Japan. He complemented those efforts with degrees in manufacturing, computer animation, and graphic design, skills he brought to Mattel in 2008.

One of Schmid's highlights to date was leading design on Hot Wheels Wall Tracks. This concept elevated the play area from the horizontal to the vertical, attaching to a child's wall. The idea, in part, was to free up floor space and create a toy that parents and kids didn't feel obligated to put away on any particular timeframe.

A wall-mounted set was radical enough that Schmid and his collaborators worked on it quietly on top of their other projects until they had a functioning prototype to present to management. In a fortuitous sign, before that meeting began, a contractor working in the building stopped in the hallway to observe the set mounted to a mock wall and said, "I want that for my son."

Refinements followed in the review process. A coworker's inquiry, "What if my dog jumps up on it?" led the team to design break-away mounts that released the set without snapping. Schmid worked with 3M—a company with some experience in creating products that safely stick to walls—to create adhesive pads that parents could remove, leaving no marks. With this innovative mounting system, Hot Wheels Wall Tracks recieved two T.O.T.Y. awards in 2012.

The team's peers in Die-cast Design haven't sat idly. Scaled speeds for Hot Wheels have nearly doubled in recent years, multiplying both challenges and opportunities for the tricks and races the cars perform.

If the pressure is sometimes stressful, the variety and camaraderie more than make up for it. Overall, it's amply satisfying work. A simple, recurring theme when Mattel's creative minds describe their job mirrors what they love to hear from customers: "It's fun."

Above: Wall tracks expanded the number of play surfaces a room could have by four—like the Hot Wheels Wall Tracks Super Combo Pack Set with other sets shown here. **Opposite:** In search of fresh play, Mattel's designers vary tracks as well as cars. Shown here is the Thrill Drivers Corkscrew Set, 1977.

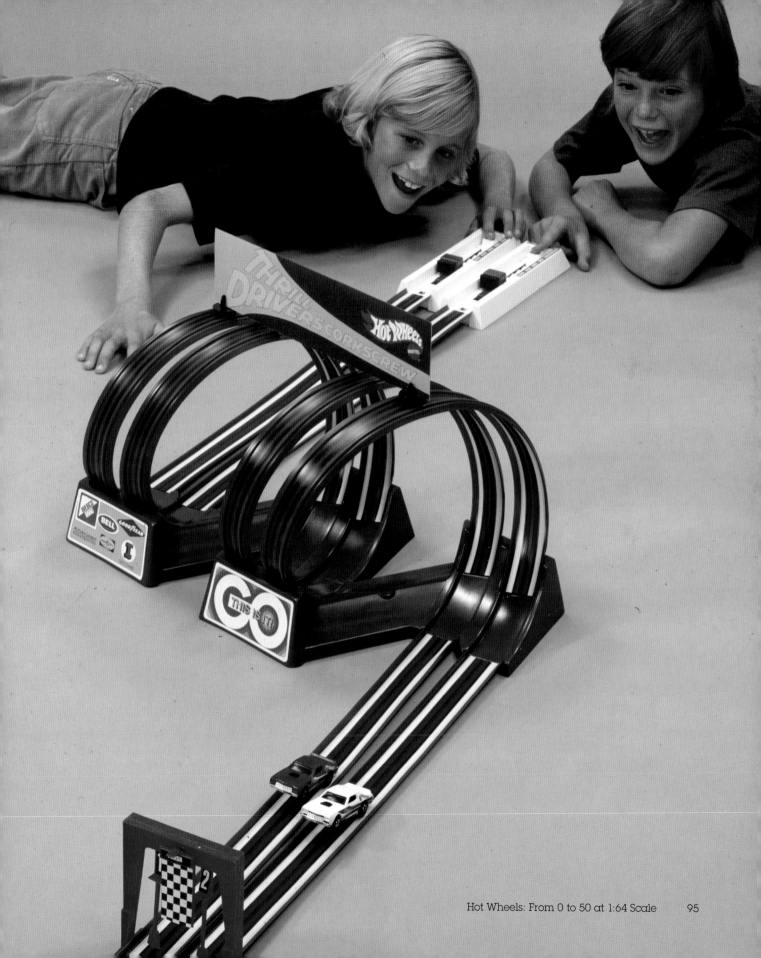

Tracks & Cases Timeline

1968 sets

Hot Wheels released its first track set: Hot Curves Race Action Set.

Daredevil Loop with its gravity-defying 360-degree loop and the Stunt Action Set with the thrilling Daredevil Loop and two jump ramps soon followed.

1970 sets

The Sizzlers California 8 Race Set debuted at the 1970 Toy Fair held in New York City. That same year the Hot Wheels Dual-Lane Rod Runner, the Drag 'chute Stunt Set, and the Mongoose & Snake Drag Race Set were released.

1968 cases

Known as the "Wheel Case," this case could hold 12 cars. Also released this year was the Pop Up Grandstand 12 Car Collector's Case with a pop-up viewing stand and tabs connect it to orange tracks.

1960s

1969 sets

The Super-Charger Double Action Set is released featuring super-charger power-boosters. Also debuting this year was the tri-level Talking Service Center play set with drive-up ramps and 10 different sound tracks.

1970s

1974 set

The release of the Flying Colors Double Dare featured a red, white, and blue-striped track for a classic drag race.

1969 cases

The 48 Car Collector's Case is released along with the classic and the Snake & Mongoose versions (not pictured here) of the Hot Wheels Collector's Race Case, each holding 48 cars.

1975 set

The stick-shifting showdown— Thundershift 500— was released.

1976 sets

Two sets—the patriotic Double Duel Speedway and the sleek Sizzlers II Silver Circuit track set—were released.

1981 set

The ever-popular Sto & Go fold-up play set was released.

1977 set

The Thrill Drivers Corkscrew set was released.

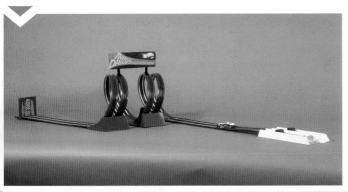

1981 case

The release of the classic 24 Car Collector's Case.

1980s

1983 set

The release of the Dash & Crash Speedway set offered side-by-side racing action.

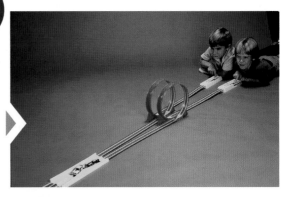

1978 set

Criss Cross Crash set introduced the intersection of the single-lane figure-eight track.

1979 set

The Wipeout Track allowed racers to crank up the speed on a double-lane, double-loop track.

1986 set

TurboTrax was released and featured glow-in-the-dark racing.

1995 sets

The colorful Top Speed play set was released with a new Daredevil Loop and the Power Loop track set which had it all—loops, gravity-defying hairpin curves, a power charger booster for the ultimate speed, and a stunt zone with real crashing action.

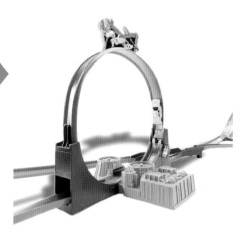

2000 case

The Hot Wheels 100-Car Rolling Storage Case was released and featured a telescoping handle.

1997 set

The Super Speedway, a battery-powered slot car race set, was released.

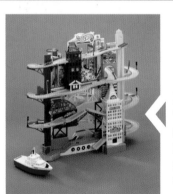

2001 sets

The gravity-defying Fireball Raceway set was released featuring nine crash zones. The Shark Park track and play set was also released this year.

1990s

2000s

1998 set

The tiered, multi-activity Uptown Downtown playset was released.

2004 sets

Playsets went to the wild side with the release of Slime Volcano and T-Rex Takedown.

1998 case

Reminiscent of the original "Wheel Case," this red and black Sto & Go Race Case held 16 cars visible through a peek-a-boo wheel-shaped cover.

2006 sets

The release of the V-Drop Super Velocity Track Set took Hot Wheels to new heights with a vertical drop. While the Terrordactyl Track Set took the action to the air.

2006 case

The Hot Wheels Rollin' 100 Car Case with removable dual launcher was released.

2007 sets

The full-service station playset, Hot Wheels Flip 'n Go Spin City, was released along with the prehistoric track set Raptor Rampage.

2009 sets

The release of Super Jump Raceway and Sharkbite Bay let cars race through an urban jungle and an island coaster.

2014 sets

Super Loop Chase Race, Shark Port Showdown, and Total Turbo Takeover were released.

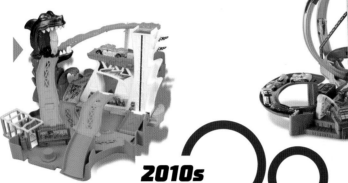

2014 cases

The Ring of Fire Stunt Case held 40 cars and featured a double-sided case with track connectors and a "ring of fire" for Hot Wheels to jump through.

2015 sets

Hot Wheels tackled the elements with the release of the Spin Storm track set and the Volcano Blast track set. The Ultimate Garage was also released making it the largest Hot Wheels garage set to date.

2010s

2011 sets

Hot Wheels launched the 4-Lane Elimination Race and the Super 6-Lane Raceway track sets allowing multiple racers to eliminate the competition. This year also saw the debut of Hot Wheels Wall Tracks, using 3M technology.

2016 set

The Track Builder System Power Boost kit was released, pushing cars to a new level of speed.

2017 sets

Speed Chargers updated the Sizzlers concept with the LED Racers Figure-8 Raceway track set. The Roto Revolution set added a new spin to head-to-head competition.

Criss Cross Crash has hairpin turns, motorized boosters, and a giant crash zone.

2012 sets

The T-Rex Takedown and Mega Loop Mayhem track sets were released, along with several track accessories such as Crane Crasher, Claw Escape, and Scorpion Gravity.

2017 case

Track Builder Stunt Box was launched to help builders create epic new Hot Wheels worlds.

LIVING HOT WHEELS

From the beginning, Mattel saw that Hot Wheels had appeal beyond just the cars. They expanded the play value by offering carrying cases and track sets, but they also saw that the brand—with its unmistakable flamed logo and vivid colors—could extended beyond direct tie-ins.

Mattel soon created consumer products that allowed kids to show off their Hot Wheels fandom in a variety of ways—from lunch boxes to wallets. They also partnered with other companies, licensing the Hot Wheels brand, to offer an even wider selection of products such as watches, bubble gum, temporary tattoos, and much more.

Hot Wheels quickly became an immersive brand, one in which kids could not only play with the cars, but also share stories and compare collections with the ever-growing Hot Wheels community.

Mattel combined storytelling and racing by launching a Hot Wheels comic book series in 1970. Mattel publishing soon grew to include Hot Wheels storybooks, sticker books, fan magazines, and collector handbooks for kids.

Over the past five decades, Hot Wheels has explored many different product types, bringing the brand to birthday parties, room decor, clothing, and other racing or car-related products—such as bikes, toolboxes and skateboards.

Hot Wheels has truly become a lifestyle brand and the supporting products have become collector's items in their own right.

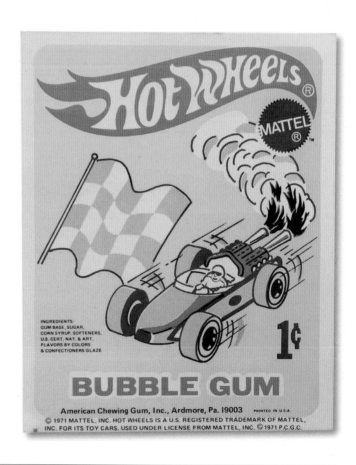

Top: Front (left) and back (right) of Hot Wheels metal Thermos lunch box, 1969.
Bottom: Rare Hot Wheels bubble gum paper, 1971.

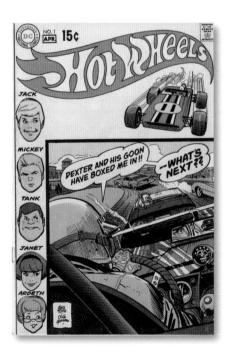

Top left: A Bradley Hot Wheels wristwatch, 1970. **Top right:** A Mattel-produced Hot Wheels wallet, 1972. **Bottom left:** The first issue of the *Hot Wheels* comic book, released 1970. **Bottom middle:** A July 2012 issue of the UK magazine *Totally Hot Wheels*. **Bottom right:** A 2016 collector's guide and handbook for kids.

Retro Hot Wheels t-shirts, 2017

Hot Wheels American Pro Car Care, 2017

Child's red Step 2 Toddler-to-Twin Car Bed,
with Hot Wheels track connectors, 2015

Retro Hot Wheels '68 Race Team Pit Crew
metal lunchbox, 2017

Hot Wheels Birthday Candles, 2017

Backpack with Hot Wheels miniature car
and keychain, 2017

Hot Wheels Illest sweatshirt
and toolbox, 2017

Hot Wheels brand skateboard, 2017

Dynacraft 16" Hot Wheels Bike, 2017

Over five decades, Mattel has explored
many different product types as
recipients for the Hot Wheels logo.
Race-themed apparel are a time-
honored medium for displaying favorite
things. Backpacks and lunch boxes can
personalize the school experience, while
Hot Wheels birthday candles tie in with
rolling gifts. The bed has prompted
adult laments that it comes only in
children's size. It connects with track on
either side, allowing some new-model
speed tests before breakfast. Bikes and
skateboards promote motion for its
own sake—and to head over to friends'
houses to play with Hot Wheels.

Ferrari F430 Challenge

Honda Civic Si

PLAYING SCALES

The Sweet Sixteen cars that launched the Hot Wheels name were ¹⁄₆₄ scale. That was the size the orange track, plus the lion's share of accessories, were designed to accommodate. But the toy market is insatiable, with new children, new trends, and new age groups emerging every year who are interested in miniature cars.

Changing scale can make a vehicle unsuitable for certain accessories or play sets. It can create advantages too. Fine details and increased complexity are easier to achieve and see with a bigger car. Fashioning and moving working doors, hoods, trunks, steerable wheels, and lifelike suspensions is also simpler with a little more finger room.

Going the other direction may also have perks. Children's hands and pockets can be quite small. Tiny cars feel specifically kid-sized and can be carried and played with in numbers appealing to youthful attention spans. When made with fewer details, such as no or minimal interior, they can also be more cost-effective to produce.

Mattel has made miniatures at ¹⁄₁₂, ¹⁄₁₈, ¹⁄₂₄, ¹⁄₄₃, ¹⁄₅₀, ¹⁄₆₄, and ¹⁄₈₇ scales. The large ¹⁄₁₂ models have included production cars, such as the C6 Corvette, as well as fictional vehicles, such as the Batcycle with sidecar, used by Batman and Robin in the original TV series. Numerous Ferrari models were built at ¹⁄₁₈ scale; Monster Jam trucks at ¹⁄₂₄; movie cars from *Back to the Future*, *Batman*, and *The Love Bug* (Herbie), and others at ¹⁄₄₃; the Scooby-Doo Mystery Machine and the *Flintstones'* Flintmobile at ¹⁄₅₀; and the Hot Wheels Micro Racers at ¹⁄₈₇.

In addition, for every adult in the fan flock—and a lot of the kids—there are many vehicles in the Hot Wheels line built at "real"-car-size, or 1:1, reduction scale: none.

Left: Mattel has released vehicles as small as ¹⁄₈₇ scale, such as this Ferrari F430 Challenge (top) and Honda Civic Si (bottom). **Right:** Mattel has also collaborated with manufacturers and customizers to build road-going vehicles like this Camaro.

Above: In between the traditional and life-size scales is a range of scales offering greater detail and more moving parts. Top row: $1/12$-scale Mustang GT 350 and $1/18$-scale Ferrari. Middle row: $1/24$-scale monster trucks; Bottom row: $1/43$-scale Herbie the Love Bug and $1/50$-scale *Flintstone* car.

REEL TO REAL

Entertainment cars are a fertile field for play and reminiscence. If there is a story that portrays a cool vehicle, or is amenable to adapting its themes into a car, odds are good that someone designing Hot Wheels for Mattel has thought of it.

Hot Wheels had long been producing cars that tied to real car brands, racing leagues, famous drivers, and commercial brands. So it was natural when Hot Wheels began pulling inspiration from TV and movies. Films and shows that feature specific cars such as *Herbie*, James Bond films, or the *Flintstones* were obvious to scale down for a Hot Wheels edition. Other films and shows have such compelling story themes and characters that finding a way to capture those elements in a car design allows fans—especially the younger ones—to re-create and expand the story's adventures.

When Hot Wheels began creating these entertainment-based cars, they were difficult to find and aimed at collectors. But in recent years Mattel has righted this injustice. In part, the designers who wanted those vehicles as children are now working at Hot Wheels and creating innovative cars inspired by movies, cartoons, comic books, and TV shows.

The Hot Wheels Entertainment lines first released in 2013 brought cars inspired by classic TV and movies popular in the '60s and '70s such as *Star Trek*, *Batman*, *The Jetsons*, *Scooby-Doo*, *Starsky & Hutch*, *The Rockford Files*, *The Brady Bunch*, *American Graffiti*, *Grease*, *Smokey and the Bandit*, *The Love Bug*, *Stripes*, and *B.J. and the Bear*.

Films and series from the '80s to the present are also available or underway, including the *Star Wars* lineup, *The Muppet Show*, *Magnum P.I.*, *Back to the Future*, *Knight Rider*, *Battlestar Galactica*, *The A-Team*, *Miami Vice*, *Beverly Hills Cop*, *Ferris Bueller's Day Off*, *Footloose*, and *Stroker Ace*.

Characters from comic books and fantasy-based story lines allowed Hot Wheels designers to combine their extreme styling skills with some of the most popular and iconic entertainment characters. Hot Wheels has produced DC Comics–based vehicles for characters like Wonder Woman, Hawkman, the Riddler, Robin, Batgirl, Ares, Superman, Aquaman, Cyborg, the Penguin, the Swamp Thing, Doomsday, and the Flash as well as Marvel-derived Hot Wheels for characters like Iron Man, Groot, Spider-Man, Captain America, Venom, Red Skull, Hulk, She-Hulk, Rocket Racoon, Doc Ock,

Rhino, Thor, the Punisher, Wolverine, Deadpool, and Loki, among others.

And, as always, Hot Wheels has created cars that capture imaginative play by pairing one of a kind styling with beloved characters and stories. For pop culture fans who love cars, real or imagined, it's a great time to be a kid—no matter what age you happen to be.

Above: Hot Wheels created scale versions of vehicles from popular TV shows and movies. Top: *Grease* '48 Ford. Middle: *Scooby Doo* The Mystery Machine van. Bottom: *The Brady Bunch* '71 Plymouth Satellite.

Above: Hot Wheels TV show and movie licensed vehicles. Top row: *Tom and Jerry* character-inspired cars. Middle row: The *A-Team* van. Bottom row: *Ghost Buster*'s vehicle, Kit from *Knight Rider*, and the *Footloose* Beetle.

Above: Hot Wheels Marvel and DC character–inspired cars. Top: Spider-Man and and Groot cars. Bottom: Superman and Wonder Woman cars.

Above: Hot Wheels *Star Wars*–inspired character and vehicle cars. Top: Darth Vader and First Order trooper cars. Bottom: Yoda and R2-D2 cars.

ONE ON ONE

All toys are real—the ones you can see and hold and step on in the dark. When you're a kid, they're more than real. The whole experience—the speedy flash of the chromed rims and shiny paint, the hum of the wheels over extruded orange track, the coolness to the touch of the die-cast bodies, even in summer . . . It's all bigger, more visceral, more engaging—as if a part of your consciousness were there in the car, staring over the hood, aware of your competitor just inches away with a shot at dropping the trip flag first.

As we grow older, our attention shifts from scale tracks to the street and the garage and the parking lot in front of a favorite burger joint. How cool would it be to have the style and power of a Hot Wheels at a size fit for the road?

That fantasy is reality as Mattel has engineered full-scale versions of several iconic Hot Wheels.

Ira Gilford designed the Twin Mill for release shortly after the Sweet Sixteen. His original seed of inspiration was super-wide tires across the back, a design that in real life would have had enormous traction. He sketched a long body, perhaps envisioning something whose front end wouldn't pop up as soon as big horses got dumped on that massive grip. So extended was this shape that it invited Gilford to dress up the space between the windscreen and the nose. Well, this was a Hot Wheels car, so what better adornment than a massive, chromed V-8—or better still, two, side by side!

Twin Mill projects space-age power, with all the custom cool of an iconic Hot Wheels hot rod. In the mid-'90s, Mattel pored over its catalog for a design to bring to full scale. This was the one that leapt out. The company hired a big-name builder and waited for the life-size toy. But the builder went bankrupt and the

Above: The life-size Hot Wheels Twin Mill on display at the Peterson Automotive Museum in Los Angeles, CA.

incomplete project was sent back to Mattel, where it sat mostly ignored until management got to thinking about Hot Wheels' thirty-fifth anniversary, happening in 2003. Carson Lev, a Mattel licensing director, got involved to finish the car and struck up a Championship Auto Shows deal with Bob Larivee Jr.—whose father had commissioned the Cushenberry Custom after which the Python was styled.

The result was fully functional and totally wicked, boasting dual supercharged 502 cubic-inch GM engines making some 1,400 horsepower. Lev has driven the car more than once, including some hot laps at Las Vegas Motor Speedway. No numbers were recorded, but the roar, the flyby, and Lev's grin suggest throttle response was something north of adequate. The car had a public debut and awed reception at the Specialty Equipment Market Association (SEMA) show in Las Vegas in 2001.

Of a different genre, Larry Wood's Bone Shaker, with its skull-face grille and headlights clutched by bony skeleton fingers, has also been enlarged. It, too, is fully functional and is used by Mattel at promotional events. Full-size cars are far more visible than their pocket-size doppelgangers.

The scale-up effort has been so successful that Mattel has brought many cars to full size, relying on the same sorts of custom builders and fabricators from places such as Southern California and Detroit that inspired the first run of Hot Wheels. Among the additional 1:1s are character cars and movie crossovers, such as the *Star Wars* Darth Vader car and X-Wing Carship; insane live-action stunt cars that navigate full-size loops and perform record jumps; a stylized new-era show car evoking the original Deora; and an actual production Hot Wheels Camaro sold by Chevrolet.

The Darth car is part of a Hot Wheels *Star Wars* mash-up that challenges our real-versus-imaginary nomenclature. It's not an actual vehicle in the sense of appearing in the films, but its design is vividly true to the Vader image. If you're jamming down a corridor for that vent on the Death Star and see this black dog in the mirror,

SCALED-UP CARS A FULL-SIZE SMASH

Top: The ¹/₆₄-scale Twin Mill shown in action on a classic track. **Bottom:** A sketch for Bone Shaker by Larry Wood shown next to its ¹/₆₄-scale version (top) and its life-size version (bottom), created by Mattel in 2011.

Above: As the maker of the world's fastest toy cars, Mattel is particularly attuned to performance. Its *Star Wars*–derived vehicles, inspired by Darth Vader (top) and the X-wing (bottom), use Corvette components to keep pace.

you know at once you've attracted the wrong trooper. There are performance Corvette parts under the custom body, including a manual six-speed transmission—yes, Darth, who hails from long ago and far away twice over, prefers to select his own gears. The X-Wing Carship is lighter and faster still, based on a Formula Ford race car. It weighs in at about 1,100 pounds and will do 160 miles per hour in Earth's atmosphere.

With the full-size stunt cars, Mattel pushed 1:1 design to its limits. The other cars are operable, even fast—but their primary purpose is display and goodwill. In the double-loop and record-jump cars, drivers' lives hang in the balance. Drops and tumbles that a ⅟₆₄-scale die-cast body can survive pose catastrophic risks at full scale. If a show car stalls or has to be pushed, that's not outside expectations. To negotiate a Ferris wheel–size loop or jump more than a football field, however, requires flawless planning and perfect execution by machine and madman.

Get on the internet and watch Tanner Foust's awesome flight in the Hot Wheels jump truck at the Indy 500 in

Above: Mattel's stunt cars are capable not only of functioning, but of setting world records—in the hands of a world-class stunt driver—such as this daredevil stunt, inspired by the V-Drop Set, at the Indianapolis 500.

2011 (a stunt aided by the design work of Alton Takeyasu). Beginning atop a giant orange hill, Foust screams down, accelerates, and jumps the vehicle 332 feet, landing and stopping in the tightest margin before space runs out. To make it, Foust needed the right speed (109 miles per hour)—fast enough to clear the gap but not so fast as to overfly the landing ramp. His vehicle also required exacting vehicle aerodynamics to keep it top up, wheels down, without rotating, tilting, or dipping its nose or tail beyond the slightest margin of error throughout its intense hang time. Then, tires, wheels, suspension design and travel, and braking all required extreme function to permit Foust to land smoothly and get all four corners settled and decelerating immediately with enough balance to avoid losing control or flipping the truck. On a test jump, Foust entered too fast, lifted off the gas, and the front of the truck dipped. It landed nose first, skidded, and went off the side of the ramp. He did not crash, but it was a hairy reminder of the near-perfect performance required.

Deora's evolutionary path would confuse even Charles Darwin. The original was in the Sweet Sixteen, based

on a full-size truck. Deora II was penned by Hot Wheels designer Nathan Proch for 1/64-scale production. In the 1990s, Mattel commissioned famed hot-rod designer and builder Chip Foose to create a life-size version.

And yes, the public can get in on the full-size game too. Chevrolet built about 1,500 Hot Wheels Camaro SS editions for 2013. Now parents and kids really can drive the same car.

Top right: The Deora II in 1/64 scale. Changes in materials allowed new shapes not previously possible on the original model. **Bottom:** Full-size version of Deora II.

Top: A full-size version of the Rip Rod vehicle. **Bottom:** The full-scale Team Hot Wheels Corkscrew Buggy that completed the record-breaking corkscrew jump. **Next page:** Hot Wheels has created a number of full-size vehicles.

Full-scale '66 Pontiac GTO.

Team Hot Wheels Monster Truck.

Full-size Bad to the Blade.

Full-size VW van in the style of Beach Bomb.

Full-size Hot Wheels Double Dare car from the Double Dare Loop in the X-Games.

A ¹⁄₆₄-scale Mustang beside the full-size Hot Wheels edition.

DEFYING GRAVITY

Looping and jumping full-size vehicles grew from the Hot Wheels for Real campaign, with which Mattel portrayed its test facility as the children's play set world brought to life. It was fabulously successful, giving kids and adults a real-world setting where drivers climbed into scaled-up toys, gazed over the hoods, and tapped full power from extreme-performance engines.

Alton Takeyasu has worked with Mattel moving scales from small to life-size and beyond. He designed the 100-foot door atop which sat the ramp for Tanner Foust's world record 332-foot jump at the Indy 500 facility. He also did the visualization design work for the double-loop that Foust and Greg Tracy ran rally cars through at the 2012 X-Games during the Downtown L.A. Takeover. The latter was a pointed example of the difference in limits between a tiny toy car and a full-size motor vehicle.

Naturally, with the jump and the double-loop, the drivers'—and onlookers'—safety were foremost concerns. Thus, subtle changes were made to the vehicles to improve visibility or create adequate suspension travel—even if it meant a slight divergence from a Hot Wheels version of the stunt car—to meet driver, engineer, and stunt coordinator demands.

These colorful wheelmen were equipped with some of the most powerful and technologically advanced stunt machines ever built—and they had to be, because of the level of risk confronted. Their stunts were performed before demanding audiences at venues including the Indy 500, where Yellow Driver (Tanner Foust) jumped a world-record 332 feet, and the X Games, where Yellow Driver and Green Driver (Greg Tracy) executed a double loop that converged on exit into a single lane. During testing for the loop maneuver, engineers first tried a remote-control car, which tumbled upside down.

Above: Much more than appearance was at stake with the double-loop stunt. It was important that spectators connect the setup with classic orange Hot Wheels track.

As with the die-cast miniature process, much of Takeyasu's foundation work for the car stunts was done with computer computations and modeling—as directed by seasoned stunt professionals. Some of the requirements ran counter to the expectations of nonexperts. For example, the drivers were concerned about too little speed, which would allow the cars to drop off the track near the top of the loop.

Testing showed that too much speed was also bad, due to the huge g-forces created by the loop. At a height of 66 feet, the circular track had a radius of thirty-three feet. Thus, over a distance of only 11 yards, the car's velocity in the *x* (horizontal) direction went from an entry speed of about 50 miles per hour . . . to zero. The force pressing Foust and Tracy into the track as it redirected that momentum from horizontal to vertical was 7Gs, a level encountered in the everyday world only by fighter pilots. Indeed, the two drivers were tested for their ability to withstand this degree of stress.

The vehicles did not have an easier time. As Takeyasu explained, the tight arc (compared to any incline a typical car encounters) was breaking the test cars' suspensions. A driverless car guided by remote control crashed when this happened and the front wheels went akimbo. While an in-car operator might have saved the stunt with the ability to react to the damage, there was no way Mattel or the drivers would take that risk. The solution was to add a couple more inches of clearance to the stunt cars and to hit the loop near the lowest speed that would retain tire contact throughout the arc. To craft a solution to a problem created by taking a toy and making it real was not something Takeyasu's education had specifically prepared him for, but he was more than up to the task. The challenge was great, but his perseverance paid off.

For Takeyasu, the toy world reached out early. He had not gone to Art Center School of Design with that goal in mind, but one of his instructors was Harry Bradley. The teacher appreciated his student's work and gave him an internship. In Bradley's studio were models of the original Deora design from the Sweet Sixteen. It was the first Mattel die-cast toy Takeyasu had owned as a child.

AT FULL SCALE

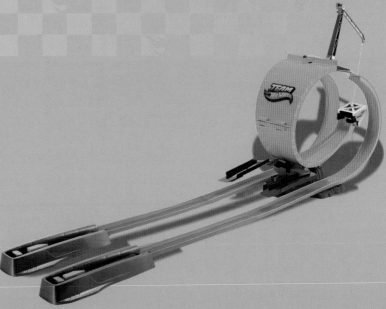

Left: This time-lapsed photo shows Foust and Tracy crushing the six-story double vertical loop at the 2012 X Games. **Right:** The Hot Wheels Double Dare Snare (2012) catches the winner in a snare. **Next Page:** Team Hot Wheels broke their third world-record in 2012 with the corkscrew jump: (top) a still of the jump, (bottom) a time-lapse photo.

SOUND AND VISION

In the early days, Hot Wheels engineers used high-speed cameras to film the cars, then slow them down, to study their movement on track. Since then, Hot Wheels have been on camera and on screen in countless contexts, showcasing their high-speed performance and play value. Further, Hot Wheels have dominated social media, with nearly nine hundred million views on the Hot Wheels channel and close to a million subscribers to the YouTube Channel.

From the start, Elliot and Ruth Handler sought the smartest, most capable people they could hire for Mattel. Their engineers were as good as any in the industry, capable of literal rocket science. And they needed to be: compared to the other die-cast miniatures that designers studied for evaluation, Hot Wheels were very fast—so fast, in fact, that it was impossible to see exactly how the cars were behaving in curves and loops and passes through the Super-Charger. To get the clear look they wanted, engineers such as Al Nash developed high-speed film techniques to study the cars in motion. In film slang, they "overcranked" the camera, shooting many more frames per second than would be typical for recording movement. This image-rich, frame-dense, footage can then be replayed slowly, providing a clear, in-focus view of the moving object because it has been captured at tiny increments of advancement.

High-speed photography showed Hot Wheels developers precisely what was happening when the cars left the track, such as in cornering or looping. It also helped the team improve the Super-Charger, by demonstrating how the foam wheels were engaging the car and its effects as the car was shot forward. Based on the slow-motion images, the engineers increased the size and softness of the padded wheels and gave them a slight downward attitude to keep the cars on the track.

Mattel has used film and broadcast media in every way possible to connect with the Hot Wheels marketplace. In 1969 the company produced an animated cartoon featuring racing themes. Many additional animated efforts have followed, including *Hot Wheels Highway 35 World Race* (2003), *AcceleRacers* (2005), *Hot Wheels Battle Force 5* (2009), and *Team Hot Wheels* (2014).

Since the advent of the smartphone—and the ubiquitous movie camera it contains—live-action Hot Wheels footage has become the dominant form by a vast margin. Today, Mattel and many of its fans

Above: Long before Hot Wheels, Mattel saw the value of television to a toy company, striking a deal with Disney to advertise on its *Mickey Mouse Club* in 1955. TV and online entertainment have grown as a way to connect with the marketplace. The animated *Team Hot Wheels* series featured (clockwise from top left) Rhett (car guru), Gage (speed demon), Wyatt (stunt man), and Brandon (gadget guy).

create content on play sets new and classic, and about collecting, restoring, and playing with Hot Wheels. Competition has led to extraordinary layouts, filling homes and lawns.

Mattel has also produced exciting, action movie-grade professional video content. It shows competitive and stunt footage as outrageous as what kids do with toy cars when little property damage and no spectacular crash-related injuries are likely. The videos feature a living Team Hot Wheels, composed of world-class professional stunt drivers outfitted as Blue Driver, Red Driver, Yellow Driver, and Green Driver.

The Yellow and Green Drivers performed world record–setting stunts at the Indy 500 and X Games (see p.118-119). Red Driver performed a few motorcycle stunts: in one he jumped over a parked jet, and in another, he hit a ramp on the back of a moving tractor-trailer and backflipped the bike into a dump truck of foam blocks passing the other way. Blue Driver added some rad driving stunts, such as drifting circles on a small round platform raised a few stories above the ground.

Though these stunts were not performed before a live audience like the Yellow and Green Driver stunts, these were tricks within the realm of a child's imagination. Thanks to vehicles engineered to Mattel's highest standards and modern cinematography from the *Fast and Furious* era, the stunts were brought to life at full scale.

Performance and innovation, combined with careful attention to Hot Wheels' millions of fans, helped propel the car from a project Mattel's own number crunchers feared could be a bust to the most popular toy on the planet. Fifty years of cars, accessories, play, and media devotion have created a complementary world to the one built by Mattel—a world of enthusiastic collectors who both celebrate what their favorite toymaker has done and create their own events, conventions, and websites.

Above: The Hot Wheels "Challenge Accepted" YouTube videos inspire fans to create extreme obstacles for their cars.

FORZA TO BE RECKONED WITH

The first Hot Wheels to hit orange track inspired a fantasy around the world: to be in that car, feeling the rush of outrageous physics, working controls, and trajectory over a soaring, sweeping raceway at the raw limits of traction and horsepower.

Fans have played out the fantasy in their minds since the debut of Hot Wheels. It's a fantasy that gave birth to live-action and animated Hot Wheels shows. But these shows created the visuals, but not the feel. Full-size Hot Wheels built for car shows offered the chance to take seat behind an actual driver's wheel—but only for a lucky few. Stunt drivers like Tanner Foust and Greg Tracy fulfilled the fantasy when they revved up real vehicles and hurled them through radical stunts on life-size orange tracks, yet only over short distances on prescribed routes and the rest of the world had to be content to just watch the action.

But on May 9th, 2017, Hot Wheels threw open the dream gates with the release of The Hot Wheels Expansion Pack in the video game racing simulator, *Forza Horizon 3*. This expansion pack for Microsoft's *Forza Horizon 3* game was

that long-imagined racer's-eye view of the Hot Wheels playscape—an epic, sprawling, speedway-in-the-sky in which you, the player, buckled up for wicked rides at exhilarating velocities.

These virtual Hot Wheels tracks rolled, swooped, and banked through giant loops, diving turns, and streaking straightaways crossing island, ocean, and urban terrain set in a gorgeous, photorealistically rendered island off the coast of Australia. Miles of track wended to the horizon with turns, intersections, AI-controlled race opponents, and some insane driving challenges, including circuit races, sprints, and stunts. There was much to explore for venturesome players, and just as much to crash into or barrel off for the unfocused gamer.

The setting was unmistakably Hot Wheels, right down to longitudinal scuffs in the orange race track that glimmer in the game's sunlight. Boost pads work like Super Chargers, launching the car with a jolt of acceleration, which can power players across seemingly impossible jumps or land the miscalculating wheel-winder into the sea. In one area, animatronic dinosaurs flash

Above: *Forza Horizon 3: Hot Wheels* Expansion Pack, released in 2016, is an open world racing video game that features cross-platform play.

toothy jaws to amp up adrenaline, and it feels perfectly at home in this rebooted dream of childlike adventures. Players race circuits or point-to-point, do jumps and stunts, and speed-camera challenges—and even modify stunt-track sections to share with fellow gamers.

Forza Horizon 3: Hot Wheels Expansion Pack also added ten special vehicles to the base game's garage. They included the iconic Twin Mill, Bone Shaker, and Rip Rod, as well as the 2005 Ford Mustang with pivoting front spoiler to clear the loop, the Jeep Trailcat—modeled after a 700-horsepower dirt monster Chrysler built to compete in a Jeep Safari in Moab—the Zenvo ST1 Danish supercar, the Toyota Hilux Arctic Truck AT38, the Pagani Zonda R, and the Chrysler VH Valiant Charger from Australia.

Playground Games developed *Forza Horizon 3: Hot Wheels* Expansion Pack for use on Xbox One and Windows 10. The developers knew that this project was guaranteed to garner huge attention for its incredible concept and stunning graphics, but the trick with a creation long-awaited is that expectations can run very high. The effort and passion for Hot Wheels paid off as *Forza Horizon 3: Hot Wheels* Expansion Pack was named top XBox One Exclusive 2017 by prestigious gaming website Metacritic.com.

All in all, the *Forza Horizon 3: Hot Wheels* Expansion Pack was a tire-squealing, engine-screaming, pulse-pushing smash from the first race day. Reviewers were delighted and fans snapped it up to speed across the cyber raceway of their dreams.

Top: Some the key players from *Forza Horizon 3: Hot Wheels* Expansion Pack are the 2005 Ford Mustang, and 2011 Bone Shaker. **Bottom:** The 2012 Rip Rod (shown here racing Bone Shaker).

HOT WHEELS

Everything that makes these die-cast miniatures the most popular of their kind derives from carefully applied science. They dust the competition on the track because the wheels and suspensions were cleverly engineered for maximum speed. Loops were possible thanks to front and rear overhangs adjusted to prevent them from dragging on sharp inclines. Design details are accurate due to skillful, proportional drafting, modeling, and casting. And the cars became available worldwide only because hordes of experts with solid science backgrounds designed and built machines, factories, and processes to permit enormous, efficient production. To dislike science is to ignore all the details that characterize Hot Wheels' capabilities.

Shortly after the cars hit the market, a Michigan physics teacher was shopping in a local toy department in search of something to engage students. His gaze fell on the Hot Wheels Stunt Action Set. A gravity-propelled car that ran over sixteen feet of track, went through a loop, and leapt between ramps was an ideal find.

The teacher, Stanley Briggs, devised four experiments to help pupils understand basic physics principles. In the first experiment—loss of energy due to friction—he created a symmetrical arc with the track going down to the ground and back up. Using two points of equal height before and after the bottom of the arc, he had students calculate how much higher than the first point (on the downhill portion of the arc) they had to release the car to allow it to reach the second point (on the uphill portion).

These calculations allowed them to determine that their particular setup (which depended on the car used and the sharpness of the arc) was 80 percent efficient—thus the car would have to be released from a height 20 percent greater on the downhill portion to reach the uphill mark.

Above: Physics and engineering expertise were essential to the beginning of Hot Wheels. The Speedometry program allows students to visualize and measure the forces acting on Hot Wheels cars as they negotiate loops, jumps, inclines, and straightaways.

That efficiency number in turn was incorporated into calculations to determine from what height the car would have to be released to navigate the loop and to clear a leap of a specific distance between the kit's ramps. In a final experiment, the class calculated how high a barrier the car could clear mid-jump. Briggs published his results in *The Physics Teacher*, concluding that his students had a high level of interest in the Hot Wheels mechanics experiments. In short, the class was engaged by the science of play.

Other teachers caught on. A pair of professors interested in middle-school math published their process for teaching kids about scale using Hot Wheels. They found that many kids this age view math only as a set of drills they're required to learn at school, not as a tool they can apply to the real world. With help from Hot Wheels, the writers helped children understand that the "1" in $\frac{1}{64}$ or 1:64 is the size of a road-going automobile and that toy cars are proportional miniatures of those vehicles. Through discussion, the pupils reached the conclusion that sixty-four Hot Wheels placed end to end would be the length of the full-size version of the same model. The teachers made sure the kids realized that the height and width of the toys should also equate to a real car by the same ratio.

The exercise permitted discussion of units of measurement and how to apply them. Their rulers had both inch and centimeter marks, and students were free to choose the one they wanted to use. They were also asked what units a scale of $\frac{1}{64}$ referred to, which led to a discussion of the units most convenient to measure a full-size car versus a miniature and the need to keep them the same when scaling up or down.

The exercises helped kids understand that science seeks precision—which may conflict with practicality at the toy level. When the class measured the Hot Wheels' actual dimensions and calculated the corresponding road vehicle's size, they found some variations from $\frac{1}{64}$. For example, a scaled-up version of the bus they were given would be only five feet tall. The kids concluded that keeping the sizing close between miniatures made packaging, shipping, and displaying the toys more efficient for Mattel and stores.

AND SPEED SCIENCE

A broader program to employ the use of Hot Wheels toy cars—such as in science, technology, engineering, and mathematics (STEM) instruction—was developed by the University of California's Rossier School of Education, with support from Mattel Children's Foundation. Called Speedometry, it teaches fourth-grade students about potential and kinetic energy, gravity, and velocity. Some cool findings have emerged in controlled tests of the program with 1,600 kids in fifty-nine classrooms in California. Children were more interested in the instruction, they performed better than control groups on tests of the same concepts, and they said it was fun.

Mattel has given away thousands of the kits to help schools explore their potential. Microsoft has also gotten involved, creating a supplemental kit that teachers and students can build and use, with sensors and software, for a deeper, digital look at the concepts involved.

Right: Data on the Speedometry program proved it successful in several ways. Students learned abstract topics more quickly, and reported more enjoyment in studying scientific concepts, compared to prior curricula.

Chapter 5

FANS FOR LIFE

Over the past five decades, Hot Wheels has captured the imagination of fans young and old. The combination of being inexpensive and widely accessible, comparatively small and lightweight and thus portable for small hands—as well as having eye-catching style—has made the brand the most popular toy in the world. And like the toy itself, its fans express their affinity in surprising ways—whether that is creating their own design riffs, pushing the limits of track lengths and obstacles, or creating their own history by becoming the ultimate Hot Wheels collector.

The Hot Wheels fan community is a vast and diverse group connected through events, conventions, and social media. There are as many ways to be a Hot Wheels fan and express that fandom as there are Hot Wheels cars. Not only do the fans follow and appreciate what the Hot Wheels designers create, fans also contribute to the brand's success, often issuing challenges and inspiring the Hot Wheels designers.

Hot Wheels cars have a universal appeal and accessibility that allows anyone to become a fan. Whether speaking to a child or to someone who is a kid at heart, you'll rarely, if ever, get a blank look when you say "Hot Wheels."

Opposite: Collectors focus on different qualities as they search for their next Hot Wheels treasure—including multiple paint schemes and variations, which this assortment of 1980's cars demonstrates. **Right:** The Boss Hoss Silver Special Mustang and display stand available to Hot Wheels Club charter members would draw most collectors' eyes as a potential rarity.

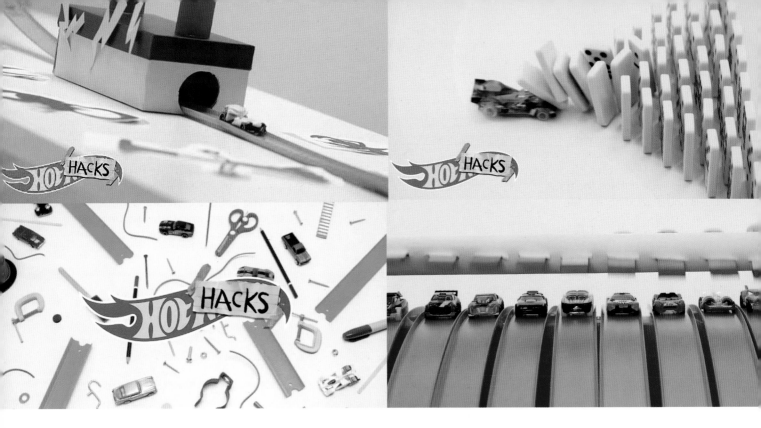

Today, Hot Wheels enjoys an advantage unimaginable in the early days of play: the existence of computers, smart phones, and social media. Platforms like YouTube, Instagram, Pinterest, and Twitter allow images and ideas to be shared instantly to anyone, anywhere.

Mattel and its fans have tapped these methods to create a robust, digital discussion about Hot Wheels and related ideas, activities, modifications, and interests involving millions of excited enthusiasts. The discussion can lead most anywhere, drawing upon cars, toys, movies, stunts, racing, nostalgia, and the vast array of products and apparel with which fans can express and share their Hot Wheels affinity.

The official Hot Wheels Instagram feed offers videos and images that extend the Hot Wheels adventures, putting the cars in scaled scenes that showcase the personality of each individually—while also offering a little Hot Wheels humor. Meanwhile the YouTube Hack the Track videos inspire new ways to explore beyond what the track sets offer and challenge the fans to create the most outrageous obstacles for their Hot Wheels cars.

Just as full-size custom shops influenced the car scene and Hot Wheels' genesis, a raft of skillful, devoted die-cast car enthusiasts have pushed perceptions of toy car style. These innovators have created various chopped, rodded, lowered, and modified cars and trucks of every form—changing engines, exhaust, paint, trim, aerodynamics, wheels, ride height, and more.

What the original designers did with a sketchpad, modern fans can do with tools, paint, donor cars, and a virtually unlimited supply of parts from production Hot Wheels, the aftermarket, and their own mini-fabrication skills. The best of these creations spread through the global fan base at the speed of thought, sustaining the dialogue and encouraging ongoing participation with feedback, Snaps, and clips of fans' own favorite concepts in the die-cast realm.

Social media makes sharing cool Hot Wheels ideas and imagery virtually effortless and instantaneous. Of course, like the actual design and production of a Hot Wheels toy, the social media creations involve sophisticated software and machinery, and require both creative and technical skills. While fans can connect with each other, Mattel also fosters the fan dialog through its design team who connect with Hot Wheels community by posting new models and styles to which fans can respond with their own unique mods, paint jobs, track setups, photography, and videos.

The size and diversity of the Hot Wheels fan base gives it a presence all its own—recognized and supported by Mattel,

Above: The Hot Wheels YouTube series Hot Hacks features the crazy stunts Hot Wheels cars can do.

with a vibrant, independent energy and creativity. Mattel and its collaborators have extended the opportunities for Hot Wheels fans to participate. The widely acclaimed video game expansion pack *Forza Horizon 3: Hot Wheels*, for example, allows players to modify portions of the circuit to create fresh challenges and share them with fellow gamers. Programs and apps, as well as the Hot Wheels tablet, provide further opportunity for digital users to program and write basic code to hack the track and enhance their Hot Wheels understanding and fun.

Hot Wheels' enormous success and appeal has also given birth to another form of fandom—the collector. Kids who played with them in their youth often saved and acquired more Hot Wheels as their budgets and priorities allowed, making many forgotten and incidental collections. Today, collectors are a large community and an essential component of the Hot Wheels phenomenon. They have meaningful relationships with the company and with one another, amassing and sharing knowledge, ideas, memorabilia, and enthusiasm. They contribute to the brand's success, suggesting new models for production, tracking and publishing collector values, hosting blogs and local and national events, and perpetuating the excitement and play value that Mattel introduced to the first generation of Hot Wheels fans.

Top: A 2016 Hot Wheels Instagram post to celebrate Father's Day. **Bottom:** Images from the Hot Wheels Instagram feed.

Above: This Hot Wheels Instagram photo of a Dodge Charger RT wishes fans a happy morning.

Above: Images from the Hot Wheels Instagram feed. Top row: A Hot Wheels Elite *Back to the Future* DeLorean with hover board; A holiday greeting from the Red Line Club. Middle row: Gas Monkey Monster Jam, 2017; Fiat 500D Modificado, 2016. Bottom row: Custom Barracuda, 2016; $^1/_{18}$-scale '66 Batmobile to honor the fiftieth anniversary of the *Batman* TV series.

"COLLECTOR"—PERFECTLY CLEAR AND TOTALLY VAGUE

It's easy to define "collector" but only in the weakest way—by using the root word in the definition: one who collects. Press any harder on the term and all form disappears. The who-what-when-where-why analysis produces different data for every single collector and collection. A person with a shoebox of fifty cars may not view it as a collection at all—only an assortment or simply "my Hot Wheels." By contrast, someone who owns only the Sweet Sixteen might consider them not only a collection but also possessions of extraordinary personal significance and value.

"Typical collector" is an oxymoron. Collectors may have common traits, while their passions and fleets have little overlap. So many different models have been produced over fifty years—more than a thousand models and many thousands of variations—that the universe of Hot Wheels may be pursued and sorted and distinguished in innumerable ways. Some fans collect only redlines, others only Treasure Hunts or fire trucks or sports cars or certain years of vehicle or particular years of manufacture. What is desirable to one collector may be of no interest to another, even if the market value is high compared to the price.

Generally speaking, collectors collect because they enjoy it, and we can be glad they do. Museums rely on collectors who cherish works they have sought and purchased and then bestowed for public appreciation. Without collectors, all manner of artistic, literary, technical, and historic artifacts would become scattered or forgotten upon the passing of their owners. Our understanding of the world is perpetuated and enlarged by this community of individuals who preserve society's creations. The same is true of the Hot Wheels collectors who supplement Mattel's archives and official publications with their own personal showcases of the toy cars they loved as children.

Above: Store displays showing off a trove of Hot Wheels were magical to kids in their day. This set appeared in stores in England, where Matchbox were the cars to beat.

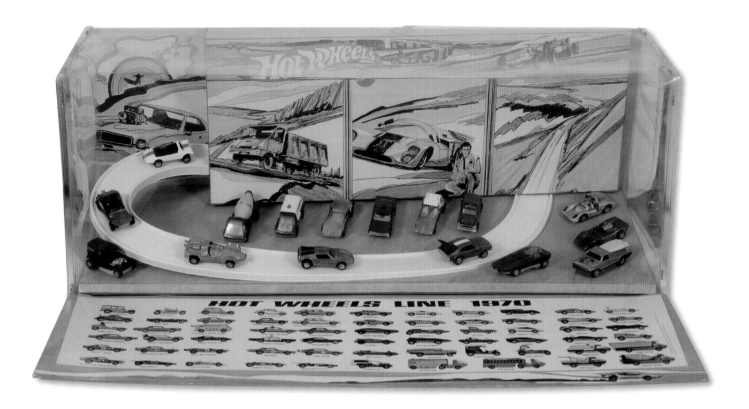

A primary reward for some Hot Wheels collectors is the memories they rekindle through acquiring toys that were important during their formative years. As adults, they have more buying power than a childhood allowance permitted and more control over the home that houses their collections. At this stage, the collection is more than playthings. Cars that increase in value and grow more difficult to find in excellent condition as the years go by may become a legacy they wish to pass on. Collectors' efforts preserve the past, the history of a toy that captivated their childhood and adult minds. They view the collection as a knowledge base and source of value.

Beyond the collection as a whole, there is excitement and anticipation in the collecting itself. Far more Indiana Joneses scour the desert than there are golden treasures. Some will score, and others will miss, as luck, timing, and detective work dictate. Finding that coveted vehicle is a thrill and a source of pride for the lucky seeker. It may bring recognition among fellow collectors and perhaps some envy from the others who were in on the chase.

Collecting is an intellectual exercise, and a creative one too. The process of deciding what to collect and gathering cars that fit the collection's goals requires research, discipline, knowledge, and careful scrutiny of available models. Variations in name, production year, color, originality, condition, and detail can produce huge swings in rarity and value. To acquire and apply the expertise required to make prudent decisions takes time, effort, and dedication.

Finally, Hot Wheels collectors enjoy the company of an ever-growing community that shares their passion and with whom they trade insights, tips, knowledge, and collectibles, while developing long-lasting friendships.

Above: This U.S. display shows the Hot Wheels available in 1970, against a backdrop of murals and open road. The murals evoke series in the lineup—Spoilers (left), Heavyweights (middle), and Grand Prix (right).

COLLECTING BASICS

Regardless of the reasons for collecting, there are a few key considerations that are important to value: rarity, originality, and condition. These criteria overlap.

The number of existing Hot Wheels of a given type has a dominant effect on value. Very limited prototypes, such as the Beach Bomb van, can fetch up to six figures. To acquire excellent examples of the original Sweet Sixteen and other desirable cars from the redline era can cost hundreds or thousands per vehicle. Simply put, the fewer collectors who can acquire a particular car, the more they are willing to pay.

Originality is important too. Hot Wheels were created as toys. As such, they met with all manner of chaos and collisions and handling and transport. Many were passed along to siblings or neighbors for more of the same. Cars lost wheels, hoods, engines, and spoilers. A quick internet search on "Hot Wheels parts" will take you to online auctions and websites selling individual components, used and new. Those items can make an incomplete car whole again, but it won't be completely original.

The car with a replacement hood or wheels is not as valuable to a collector as one in otherwise equal condition bearing all of the parts and the paint with which it left the factory. Subtle differences to the color or amount of wear or style may indicate a swap-out. In other cases, an unexpected color or wheel could indicate a variation that actually increases value. Research and logic are important tools when something looks different.

Wear and discoloration are not the only facets of condition. There are hobbyists who restore Hot Wheels—some doing an exceptional job. But a restored car is far less valued by collectors than one whose superb finish is original. As with a full-size auto, a high-quality restoration is easier if parts are separated to paint them. Thus, one sign of restoration is that the rivets on the bottom of the car do not look original—e.g., they appear too shiny or differ in size and shape from a similar example. All four wheels with utterly flawless chrome is another potential indicator. Even cars still in their original blister pack sometimes show a little wear where the chrome finish contacted the enclosure.

Finally, the condition of the vehicle in question directly affects its value. Chipped paint, damaged or misaligned logos, scratches, gouges, or any other

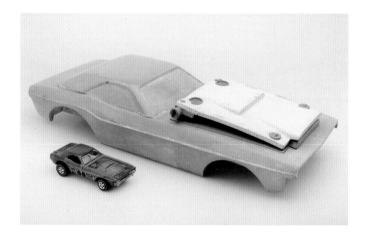

Above: Larger-scale production models are highly collectible, and no longer made. Top: The Rolls-Royce Silver Shadow was an Ira Gilford design produced in 1969. Middle: Howard Rees designed the Mighty Maverick, released in 1970. Bottom: Larry Wood's Bye-Focal (1971) was a Dodge Challenger–based vision with a stretched transparent hood.

evident wear, discoloration, or damage reduces the vehicle's value compared to another otherwise identical Hot Wheels car. Dissimilar cars cannot be used for price comparisons nor can different colors of the same model. Some shades are rarer and more desirable than others, and a rare color in one model may not be unusual in another.

A little leeway is appropriate for the early cars, particularly the Spectraflame models. An original Beatnik Bandit, Custom Camaro, or Silhouette with some minor discolorations or a little wear on the wheel chrome still has value to collectors. Those minor flaws affect more the final price than whether the car is worth owning. The older the car, the more likely it is to have some imperfections. Mattel applied the paint over plated zinc bodies to give the cars a bright, attractive shine. Variations in the alloy composition, in exposure to other substances in the factory, and to differing atmospheric conditions in the many years since production can cause areas of discoloration that collectors call toning or

mottling. This typically creates darker areas in the finish. Because the issue lies below the paint, it cannot be wiped away, and efforts to do so will create additional problems. A less common problem, also linked to a flaw in early castings, is crumbling, or disintegration of the die-cast alloy.

These are general rules addressing monetary value. Personal value can—and perhaps should—be more important. Restoring Hot Wheels can be a fun pastime, while there are also hobbyists who customize them, adding different parts, colors, or logos to their liking.

Given the billions of Hot Wheels made in many thousands of models and variations, providing individual prices is a rare skill that requires intense study. Moreover, in the internet age, values can change swiftly. Today, the collector market includes websites, blogs, and numerous publications devoted to both the vehicles and their accessories. An entire world of Hot Wheels collectors has developed around these tiny car creations, all focused on a different kind of play value.

Above: These resin prototypes and pre-production cars are other highly collectible rarities. Clockwise from top left: a resin for a Dream Station Wagon that was planned and blueprinted, but never released; a resin for the Ford Cyclone, never released; a handmade brass car used to show for catalogs and testing before the car was made for molds (actual car released in 1971); and a handmade resin classic of the '32 Vicky.

ODDITIES, RARITIES, PROMOS, & GIFTS

While personal attachment may be the strongest connection a collector has with a particular car, many other factors play into collectibility, including the way the car entered the market. Some of the most desirable cars never hit stores, only the collector market years later.

In the beginning, before there were production Hot Wheels to draw from, engineers and designers mocked up ideas with the random parts they could lay hands on—demo castings, Frankensteins of others' products with handmade additions, low-volume test runs of wheels, suspension parts, or chassis. These crude test mules had little aesthetic value and were inferior in looks and performance to the refined, quality-tested examples that reached stores. After they'd served their investigative purpose, they were tossed in a drawer or cabinet as their creators moved further down the path toward producing a consistent, high-quality toy for sale.

Some of these rough-ups were discarded or lost as facilities and staff changed. Some were pirated of parts for later tests of another idea. Still others survived—physical references of design evolution small enough to lose in the back of a drawer. Eventually, these working models resurfaced. Time and increasing interest in Hot

Wheels flushed them out of their makers' or children's hands and into the collector consciousness, where these early stepping stones have garnered revered status and top dollar.

Such oddities are rare or even unique, available to a miniscule number of collectors. Thus, most Hot Wheels in people's collections are production models. Among these are many standouts, widely known to the hobby scene. They include models from The Hot Wheels Club, Treasure Hunt, Red Line Club, and Collector Series, plus other unusual vehicles released as promotional items and gifts.

Mattel created the Hot Wheels Club for 1970. With the coupon and a buck, a child received a membership kit with Hot Wheels racing stickers, a club patch, membership card, color catalog with the 1970 lineup, and a special car with a chrome finish. Ads tended to mention the Boss Hoss Mustang, but a Camaro named Heavy Chevy and a Plymouth Barracuda tagged King Kuda were also available. These chrome cars came with a white or black plastic interior and were not available outside of the club. The program was targeted at children, perhaps with help from a parent filling out the form and mailing it.

Above: This Camaro has the open engine bay and exposed, blown V-8 of the Heavy Chevy (1970) but without the black grille. Door number and roof stripes look ill-fitting, while front wheels look barely worn. The windshield is clear, rather than tinted blue. This one deserves a closer look as a low-production/early oddity. A Mattel employee kept this model, never released in gold.

By the 1990s, a generation had passed since the introduction of the Original Sixteen. Parents who had had Hot Wheels as kids began to notice them again when shopping for toys for their own children. Buying the cars for their young ones prompted a renewed interest by adults in this standout chapter of their own childhoods. The thrill spread beyond parents as adults of all ages began collecting in earnest, whether or not they had little ones at home. Mattel decided to point a line of vehicles directly at this enthusiastic crowd.

The Treasure Hunt series was introduced in 1995 with the adult collector in mind. Because these cars were aimed at collectors, more likely to protect and display the cars than jump and crash them and run them through Super-Chargers, Mattel fitted some of these cars with authentic-looking Real Rider synthetic rubber tires. Mattel has made subtle variations to the Treasure Hunt cars and packaging over time, including a substantial change in 2007. That year, Super Treasure Hunts were introduced, with much lower quantities and different features to distinguish them from mainline models—the standard production run—and from other Treasure Hunts.

Top left and right: The Hot Wheels Treasure Hunt Red Line Cub master set of die-cast cars, case front and interior. **Bottom:** An overhead view of "Boss Hoss" Custom Mustang from the 2008 Red Line Club in Spectraflame blue.

Science Friction®

○ Metal Flake Paint
□ Wide White Walls
☆ New Paint Style
◇ Moving Part
† HiRAKERS®
‡ Pop-Up Body

#4356 Cadillac Seville ○

#4361 Bywayman® ○

#4339 Up Front 924 ○

#3362 Chevy Citation ○

#4340 Sunagon ○

#4364 BMW M1 NEW '83

#4360 Baja Breaker® ○ ◇

#4373 Street Rodder

#4363 380 SEL ○

#4350 Super Scraper™

#4017 Peterbilt™ Dump Truck NEW '83

#4371 P-928

#4368 Beach Patrol™ NEW '83

#4353 Dodge D-50 ○ †

#4359 Race Bait 308® ○

#4358 A-OK® NEW '83

#4355 Bronco 4-Wheeler

#4351 40's Woodie™ ○ †

#4366 Formula Fever™

#4367 '40's Ford 2-Door NEW '83

#4369 Classic Cobra® NEW '83

#4365 Turbo Streak™ NEW '83

REAL RIDERS™ Vehicles
New for 1983! Twenty-four Hot Wheels®
with tires that look and feel like the real
thing! Look for the Goodyear name in
white letters!

#4352 3 Window '34® ○ †

#4372 Malibu Grand Prix

#4357 '57 T-Bird

#4354 Split Window '63® ○ †

80

Above: White-letter tires were hot in the '70s and '80s, a look Real Riders brought
to the fore.

In 1996 the company launched a series called Hot Wheels Collectibles. The focus, again, was the collector rather than the hard-playing child consumer. These cars feature more individual parts, greater detail, and a higher price than the regular lineup.

Red Line Club followed in 2002, tapping internet fandom to link hobbyists to one another and Mattel through a website, HotWheelsCollectors.com. The club offers special cars and deals to members, including reprises of early vehicles, such as the chrome Camaro that original Hot Wheels Club members could purchase. As the name suggests, many of the membership cars wear redline wheels. Club members also get the chance to vote on new Hot Wheels they would like to see Mattel produce.

Outside companies have been responsible for additional rare and desirable variations, working with Mattel to produce promotional vehicles. Dozens of outside entities have used Hot Wheels to promote themselves, contracting for runs of several thousand to tens of thousands of vehicles. These special versions or their packaging may bear a company's name, or the models may be available solely through a purchase or offer from a company.

There have also been models made for Mattel's employees. Longtime designer Larry Wood created some custom examples for his colleagues as a gift in the mid-1970s. He handed that first one out to about fifteen people. The cars were so well received that he did more the following year. Like the outside promotional vehicles, these exclusive in-house vehicles are hard to come by and of keen interest to the collecting scene.

Above: A web address at the bottom of the package marks this Nova as a car not from the original redline era. It's from the Neo-Classics, Series 5, from 2006, limited to 11,000 examples. Released in 2015, this Red Line Club Series 13 Real Riders '83 Chevy Silverado is one of 4,000 made.

BRUCE PASCAL

Bruce Pascal's grandfather worked for the National Archives, documenting the nation's relationship with the automobile. It was more than a job; it was a calling, employing a fascination that animated his waking and sleeping thoughts throughout his life. The elder Pascal loved cars beyond explanation, acquiring ten thousand auto-related items for his home. In 1962 he passed the collection to his children, who then boosted it to seventy thousand pieces.

This is Bruce Pascal's lineage. It's in his genes. He has collected since he was a child, with a focus and energy as though his survival depended on it. In a sense it does. Pascal is a *collector*, versus a person who collects. He can't remember a time when he was not collecting something—stamps, coins, presidential memorabilia.

Pascal loves the automobile, like his grandfather and his parents before him. He once developed a fixation on the Tucker, the futuristic car whose creator believed he could displace industry giants. Pascal stormed in like Scotland Yard, hunting down objects tied to the marque—license plates, engine stamps, the company's original articles of incorporation.

Hot Wheels hit the market when Pascal was the perfect age to appreciate them as toys. They pulled him into the play world, where he raced and looped and jumped the cars and amped them up with Super-Chargers. He exhausted long days at the track he built in orange plastic.

Then life moved on, and so did he. His little Mattel hot rods and customs went into a box in his room. They were his cars, stowed away, so they did not enter the automobilia collection begun by his grandfather and expanded by his parents. Instead, they sat in their shoebox time capsule as he matured into adulthood.

Above: Hot Wheels collector Bruce Pascal with his priceless collection of Hot Wheels cars and memorabilia.

THE COLLECTOR GENE

Eventually, as parents do, they summoned Pascal to remove his childhood things to his own home. Not until the lid was off did the contents of that box hit home—like a tsunami. Each vehicle he rediscovered added to the flood of positive energy and memories inspiring a new passion. "This is it!" Pascal realized. "This is what I am going to collect!"

With other collectibles, he had gotten in and out, securing the prizes and moving on. That was not his trajectory with Hot Wheels. Other collections were flirtations and flings. This was the long-haul relationship.

Not a week later, he ran an ad in the *Washington Post*, inviting Hot Wheels owners to give him a call and turn their former playthings into cash. Within the month, he read that someone had just paid the highest amount ever recorded for one of Mattel's die-cast miniatures: $72,000, for a pink Beach Bomb van, styled after a '60s

VW bus with surfboards protruding out the rear window. It was in incredible condition, one of two pink ones known to exist—the better of the two. The model was produced only as a prototype and sent back for redesign when it performed poorly on the track and with the Super-Charger.

Pascal felt strangely cheated that he had not known about this opportunity. To him, seventy grand felt undervalued. Everyone was familiar with Hot Wheels; surely there were other collectors whose fire burned with an intensity close to his own. Wouldn't these people see extraordinary value—six-figure value, or seven—in a pristine, wicked-cool prototype of which only two were made in a color? He resolved to track down the buyer and have a conversation. That buyer's surname was not uncommon, however, and Pascal couldn't zero in quickly. So he called the writer of the article that broke news of

Above: The famous pink Beach Bomb van sold for $72,000.00—the highest amount ever recorded for a Hot Wheels car.

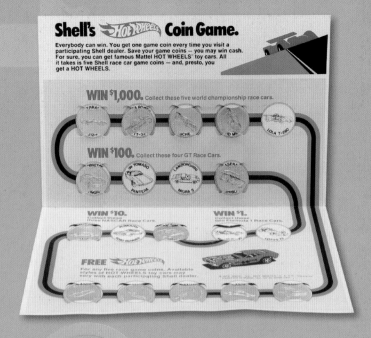

the sale. The journalist passed Pascal's number along and proved his instincts correct. There was a deal to be made—and Pascal made it.

The famed Beach Bomb is his biggest trophy, but many others have joined its ranks as Hot Wheels have shaped his life and home. He seeks a narrow band of the rare and unique—vehicles and materials related to the beginning of Hot Wheels up to 1971, the years of his childhood devotion.

Every piece has a history reaching back to its creation and progressing through its one or many owners. Pascal finds a point on that timeline, working forward to the present with the car currently in hand and then backward to gather its storied past. A pivotal find for his treasure hunt was an employee handbook for Mattel, dated 1970. That key alone helped him unlock the human history of his favorite toy and make contact with some four hundred former workers. The facts and mementos they helped him find are invaluable to his collection and contentment.

Although Hot Wheels are not his living, the archivist's grandson does work from a desk that celebrates his obsession. It was designed by an architecture firm from a specific direction—what the office of Mattel's president might have looked like in 1970. The office is not a reproduction; it's a tribute, with broad overhead beams styled like orange track arching over a glass desk showcasing bits of his collection—which he rotates for fresh inspiration.

Prior collections held Pascal's interest for a year or two before his restless mind moved on. The hobby was right, but not the focus. The box at Mom and Dad's, retrieved as an adult, put him on the proper path. Hot Wheels merge the wonderment of youth with Pascal's love of the chase. To Pascal, Hot Wheels are more than a collection. They have become his life's passion. And he is far from the only collector to experience that particular devotion.

Above: Corporate collaborations can advance two companies at once. This Whitman book of Hot Wheels stickers (left) was designed to sell the book and the cars it featured. Many businesses, including Shell, used Hot Wheels to promote themselves through logos or special offers to acquire the cars like this Coin Game from Shell (right).

Top: Displays and packaging used for other countries are also fun collectibles, as are rare colors and variants with unique features and histories, like this one from Japan, 1978. **Bottom left, right:** An assortment of 1980s Hot Wheels.

A COMMUNITY LARGE AND SMALL

With their low price and huge variety, Hot Wheels are accessible throughout the world. People of all backgrounds and nations own and enjoy Hot Wheels. The miniature vehicles are a point of shared interest for hundreds of millions of people, which creates limitless opportunity for gatherings with a few fans over coffee or thousands at a national convention.

Conventions in many countries have begun as smaller gatherings of enthusiasts. They meet to enjoy the stories and camaraderie, then disband, eager to talk about the fun they had and plan the next meet-up. Word spreads fast, and other fans want in on the action. This exponential growth has resulted in annual national conventions in the United States since 1996 and has prompted conventions in other nations, such as Japan, Mexico, and Brazil, as collectors have gathered the critical mass to make such an event a success.

The U.S. convention, for example, features special, limited-edition Hot Wheels that only registrants, or those who win contests at the convention, can obtain. The small group of collectors lucky enough to acquire these special editions almost never part with them, and when they do, the limited availability of these special cars creates instant demand and high prices.

Top: Enthusiasts gather to look at a collection of die-cast cars at the 2017 Hot Wheels Annual Collectors Convention in Los Angeles, California. **Bottom:** Fans enjoyed sitting in a life-size version of a Hot Wheels X-Wing Fighter at the San Diego Comic-Con in 2016.

Above: The ribbon-cutting ceremony kicks off the Annual Mexico Hot Wheels Convention in 2017.

MICHAEL ZARNOCK

Reclining in the Batmobile, staring out its parabolic windscreen down its long black hood, Michael Zarnock realized that his love of Hot Wheels had served him well. But this was no dream about to end with the alarm clock. Adam West had actually sat here. Famed car customizer George Barris was present now. Barris was talking about the caped crusader's ride and then about the Munster Koach, which Zarnock sat in next. It wasn't even a tour—just a visit with a friend, an iconic figure from Zarnock's childhood he had come to know through Hot Wheels.

Zarnock traces his affection for Hot Wheels to a particular bike ride in 1968. He had pedaled down to W. T. Grant's discount department store to have a look at the toys in the window. He was a born car nut, with models and Matchbox—whatever he could get. His father was an auto mechanic, and toy cars were an obvious purchase for his son. Michael had seen nothing like this, though.

In the window at Grant's, there were brightly colored toy cars with wicked engines and mag wheels. They looked fast and ferocious sitting still. He bought a Beatnik Bandit, or a Silhouette—he's not certain which was first—and the die was cast. He collected voraciously until he was about twelve or fourteen years old. At that time, he asked a friend whether he had seen the new Hot Wheels Corvette. The friend gave him a funny look and asked, "What? You collect Hot Wheels? What are you, a little kid?"

Zarnock was hurt. He kept quieter about his collection, and other considerations grew to dominate his life, like marriage, a house, and a son. It was the son, in fact, who got Zarnock back to full-throttle acquisition when the tyke began playing with toy cars. Dad met other adult collectors and they became friends, sharing tips and stories. They would accompany their kids to the

Above: Michael Zarnock's fascination with Hot Wheels led to an extensive expertise as he set about documenting and collecting cars bearing unique features that had gone mostly unnoticed by the collector world.

toy stores and scope out the new models. He found a fellowship with like-minded adults. Almost all collectors played with the cars, he said. "It's the play that created the love, the passion."

With his early collecting, Zarnock was going for one of every casting, but a fellow collector would point out subtle differences. "This one has a different wheel," he'd say, or "this interior is a different color." With eyes now opened to alternate possibilities, Zarnok was inspired to add variations to his collection goals. The variants sent him seeking books that might address their rarity or value, but nothing turned up. Stymied, he began to catalog the differences himself.

In the 1990s, his wife purchased a computer. When an IT person came over to set it up, Zarnock expressed skepticism. The installer asked him what he was into, and Zarnock answered, "Hot Wheels." The technician did an internet search, and links to Hot Wheels information popped up on the screen. "Whoa," thought Zarnock. "This could be good."

Using the internet, his own resources, and those of his friends, Zarnock created a website devoted to Hot Wheels variations. He took emails and answered questions, and many people asked for his list. He sent it, repeatedly. Then Mattel would release more cars and more variations, and the work continued. Staying on top of everything was a big job—and so far, an unpaid one. He wondered whether a publisher would be interested and queried a few.

Krause Publications said yes, and *Hot Wheels Variations* went to press. Then something unexpected happened. His acquisitions editor wanted another book. Zarnock hadn't pitched anything and didn't have a manuscript. The editor was persistent, though. He was after a price guide, so Zarnock followed through. The print run sold out immediately. More books followed—accessories, prototypes, field guide—plus articles for magazines. Zarnock was a devoted expert, and the collector community was eager for his input.

He attended his first convention in 2002. Fans knew his website, bought his book, and asked for his

LIVING THE DREAM

Above left: Michael Zarnock poses with Tom Daniel at a Hot Wheels convention.
Right: Zarnock's world records on display at his home.

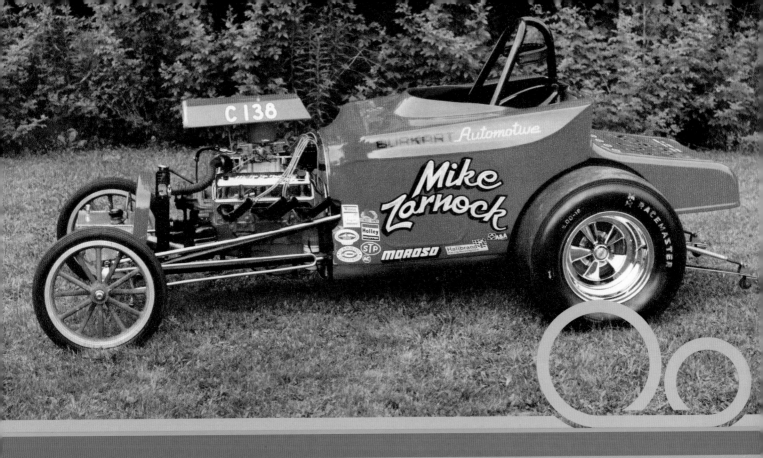

autograph. They wanted his insights on collecting. He continued with the writing and the convention scene.

At a big die-cast event in Las Vegas, promoters directed him to a table, where famous customizers George Barris and Tom Daniel were sitting. There was a seat between them—for Zarnock. He couldn't believe it. "It was one of the most amazing days of my life," he said. "These guys were my idols, and here's Tom Daniel on my right, George Barris on my left." Zarnock sat and signed autographs with them and they talked. Zarnock's expertise and enthusiasm won the customizers' respect, and they became friends. He ate dinner after the show with actress Catherine Bach, whom he knew better by her character's name, Daisy Duke.

Other high points would follow. His passion put him at events with Larry Wood—today also among his friends. This is a benefit of conventions, he noted. The big names in Hot Wheels history—both Mattel employees and tangential personalities—are present and accessible. Wood regularly invites people back to his shop to see the many fascinating fruits of his labors, from full-size hot rods, which he builds to

this day, to artwork and prototypes from his amazing tenure at Mattel.

Zarnock's devotion has brought him other honors too. He has held two world records in the *Guinness World Records* book for the size of his collection—between twenty thousand and thirty thousand Hot Wheels. Perhaps best of all, Mattel included him in the lineup itself, in the 2009 Drag Strip Demons series. A red version of the *Altered State* die-cast car is a tribute to a real dragster Zarnock raced in the northeast in the 1980s, emblazoned with Zarnock's name on the door in the same font. Including Zarnock in the series puts him in the company of further heroes—drivers such as Don Prudhomme, Tom McEwen, Bruce Larson, and Sox & Martin.

And all of it flowed from a toy he saw in the window as a boy. It's a time he still remembers so clearly. His driveway was always full of orange track, and he'd be out there playing with the cars. A neighbor kid would wander by and say, "I have Hot Wheels." Zarnock was always ready with the same challenge: "Go get 'em. We'll race."

Above: An original Loggne chassis car built for Carl Heichel, who raced it as "Carole's Mink" before Michael Zarnock obtained it and transformed it into the '23 "T" Roadster.

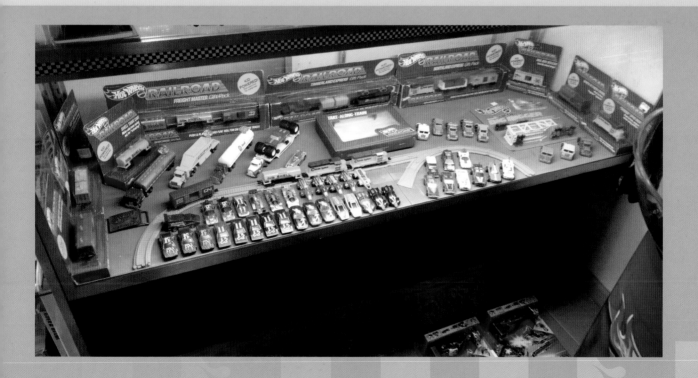

Above: Just a small sample of Michael Zarnock's extensive Hot Wheels collection.

Ultimate Hot Wheels Timeline

1967

Car designers Fred Adickes and Harry Bentley Bradley join the Hot Wheels team along with Artist Rick Irons, designer of the original Hot Wheels logo (p. 75).

Ken Sanger orders 50 million Hot Wheels for Kmart stores (p. 25).

1969

Engineer Jack Malek proposed using the mandolin wire for Hot Wheels car axles (p. 32).

Designer Larry Wood joins the Hot Wheels team (p. 42).

1971

Hot Wheels receives its U.S. patent for "Curved Track Section for Miniature Toy Vehicles" (p. 51).

1960s

1970s

1968

Mattel introduces the first die-cast Hot Wheels vehicles, dubbed the "Sweet Sixteen" (p. 36) as well as its first four race sets—the Strip Action Set, the Stunt Action Set, the Drag Race Action Set, and the Hot Curves Race Action Set (p. 48–50).

1970:

Mattel sponsors its first drag racers, Don "the Snake" Prudomme and Tom "the Mongoose" McEwen and releases their Snake and Mongoose funny cars (p. 52–55).

1972

Mattel eliminates the collector's button.

The company's manufacturing is moved to a facility in Penang, Malaysia, and raises the million-a-week production mark to a million a day (p. 70–73).

1973
The Spectraflame paint is discontinued (p. 82).

1974
Hot Wheels puts the tampo print process into full production (p. 78-79), and also begins using the "Flying Colors" slogan (p. 79).

1977
Redline wheels are phased out (p. 66).

1981
Hot Wheels introduced a thinner wheel and axle to increase speed in the Hot Ones line (p. 86).

1988
The magic of Color Changers hits the scene (p. 83-84).

1980s

1983
Hot Wheels introduced Real Riders, which featured real rubber wheels (p. 139).

1979
Hot Wheels introduces Scene Machines.

1989
Mattel moves its headquarters—including its Hot Wheels team—from Hawthorne to El Segundo, CA (p. 67).

1993
Lead Designer Phil Riehlman joins the Hot Wheels team (p. 42). Hot Wheels moves away from wood and clay modeling in favor of 3-D computer modeling (p. 58).

2001
Twin Mill becomes the first full-scale version of a Hot Wheels car (p. 110).

2002
Hot Wheels launched its exclusive online Red Line Club for serious collectors (p. 141).

2006
Hot Wheels collector Bruce Pascal purchases the pink 1969 Volkswagen Beach Bomb, now valued at a million dollars (p. 143).

1990s

2000s

1995
Hot Wheels introduces the Model series and Treasure Hunt series (p. 139).

1996
The Hot Wheels Collectibles series was launched (p. 141).

1997
Hot Wheels partners with NASCAR (p. 52).

2003
Michael Zarnock earns a Guinness World Record title for having the largest Hot Wheels collection (p. 150). Hot Wheels partners with DC Comics and releases a Batmobile miniature (p 41).

1999
Hot Wheels parners with Monster Jam (p. 104).

2005
Hot Wheels premieres its AcceleRacers series of animated films (p. 122).

2007
Hot Wheels released its first 1/87-scale cars, which were produced for only three years. (p. 104).

2009
The reissue of designer Larry Wood's 1975 *Ramblin' Wrecker* is released and Larry Wood retires from Hot Wheels (p. 42).

2010
Toy Story character cars are introduced.

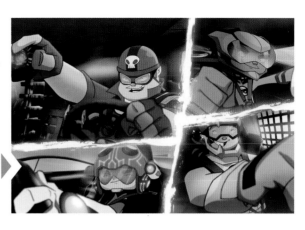

2014
Mattel releases the animated film, *Team Hot Wheels* (p. 122) and the first *Star Wars* Character Cars hit the store shelves (p. 109).

2011
Tanner Foust takes flight in the Hot Wheels jump truck at the Indy 500 (p. 113), and the innovative Hot Wheels Wall Tracks are released (p. 94).

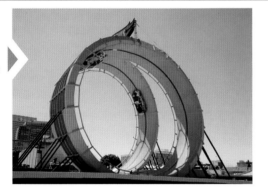

2016
Hot Wheels launches a YouTube channel (p. 130).

2010s

2012
Hot Wheels joins the X-Games in Los Angeles, California, and executes the double-loop (p. 118) and also breaks the Corkscrew Jump Record in a Hot Wheels buggy (p. 118–120).

2017
In partnership with Microsoft, Hot Wheels releases the Xbox Hot Wheels Bundle in game integration with Forza Horizon 3 (p. 124) as well as an augmented reality digital app, Hot Wheels Track Builder Tango.

2013
Mattel launches its Hot Wheels for Real campaign (p. 118).

2018
Hot Wheels celebrate its fiftieth Anniversary and creates a commemorative Camaro, both at life-size and 1/64 scale.

Hot Wheels 50th Anniversary

For fifty years, Hot Wheels has challenged the limits of performance and design—and they're just getting started. The year 2018 marked the launch of several multi-year initiatives that will continue to ignite the challenger spirit in kids, fans, and collectors for generations to come.

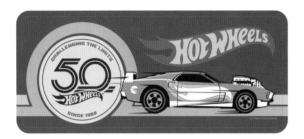

Tesla Roadster Space X Launch

In February 2018, Space X launched its Falcon Heavy rocket topped with a cherry red Tesla Roadster complete with a 1/64-scale Hot Wheels version of the roadster on its dashboard.

New York Toy Fair

Hot Wheels Super Ultimate Garage wins the Toy of the Year Award in the Playset Category.

50th Anniversary Camaro

Hot Wheels partnered with General Motors to create a custom life-size Camaro in three models.

Hot Wheels Challengers

Hot Wheels champions up-and-coming athletes in skate, BMX, and karting through competitive events and content.

Legends 50th Anniversary Tour

To celebrate the 50th anniversary, Hot Wheels launched a fifteen-city tour looking for the "Sweet 16." The winner was made into a die-cast car sold at retail.

50th Anniversary Collection

Hot Wheels went all out to mark their 50th anniversary with ten new collections of anniversary cars.

Hot Wheels Team

The 2018 Hot Wheels team.

ACKNOWLEDGMENTS

Over their fifty-plus years of development and manufacture, Hot Wheels have touched billions of lives around the world. We couldn't speak to everyone. Even if we had, and wrote only one word from a person affected by each of the more than four billion cars sold, the double-spaced manuscript would have been sixteen million pages long. Publishing specs were shorter.

Among the billions affected, tens of thousands of workers have contributed to Hot Wheels' production and success. Their stories are meaningful, and any that are omitted result from logistics, not from any implication that their memories and contributions are unimportant.

If you have a loved one, family member, former Mattel employee, or dear friend who shared tales of their development or sales or marketing or collection with you, thank you for sharing the stories and keeping them alive, and thanks to them for their devotion and enthusiasm. Our regrets for any not printed here.

Further, some words must appear before others by writing and reading convention. Equal thanks to all contributors, regardless of where mentioned herein.

At Mattel, the largest toy company on Earth, enthusiasm was high for this project. People were generous with their time, their insights, and their good nature. They love what they do. They love bringing joy to children and adults with their labors. Warmest thanks to Geoff Walker, Chris Down, Ricardo Briceno, Larry Wood, Phil Riehlman, Jun Imai, Brendon Vetuskey, Paul Schmid, Alton Takeyasu, Manson Cheung, HS Lee, Scott Goodman, Lynn Sogi, Michelle Dieudonne, Deniese Britton, Kirstin Tolentino, Ambika Suppiah, for their thoughts and assistance on this big, busy, beloved company. Robin Gerber's book, *Barbie and Ruth*, provided additional well-crafted background on Mattel, its founders, and its ways.

Thanks to Mattel's Global Publishing team: Charnita Belcher, Ryan Ferguson, Kim Huven, Kristine Lombardi, and Debra Mostow Zakarin. Thank you to Vickie Cerrito and Eliana Ruiz of the Mattel Archive team. Additional thanks to Bryan Benedict, Charisse Eickhoff, and Dana Koplik of Mattel. Additional editorial, design, layout, photography, graphics, and production thanks are due to Zack Miller, Paul Ruditis, Scott Richardson, Farley Bookout, Delia Greve, Alyssa Lochner, and Tom Miller.

For reflections and assistance on the racing world, thanks to Tom McEwen, Don Prudhomme, Lynn Prudhomme, Robert Achs, Ken Achs, and Bill Doner. Bruce Pascal and Michael Zarnock provided deep and invaluable insights on the collector world and their own experiences within it and path to it. Curtis Paul from www.redlinewheels.com, Hot Wheels books by Randy Leffingwell, Angelo Van Bogart, and Mac Ragan also provided inspiration and information on Hot Wheels, Mattel, collectors, and collecting. The Mattel folks, who also enjoy working with and for collectors added their own thoughts too—thank you.

Finally, thanks to Calvin Pevon, and Keith and Pamela Moore, for a quiet dinner in St. Paul early in this project, and their inspirational memories and comments on what Hot Wheels mean to a parent and a child.

Opposite: Hot Wheels Cockney Cab sitting on a track, ready to roll.